SPORTSPERFORMANCE

CYCLING

ENDURANCE AND SPEED

MICHAEL SHERMER
Foreword by ERIC HEIDEN

D1739094

CONTEMPORARY
BOOKS, INC.
CHICAGO • NEW YORK

Library of Congress Cataloging-in-Publication Data

Shermer, Michael.
  Cycling: endurance and speed.

  1. Cycling.   2. Bicycle racing.   I. Title.
GV1041.S5   1987   796.6   87-6721
ISBN 0-8092-4775-5

Photos by Michael Coles unless otherwise noted.

Copyright © 1987 by Michael Shermer
All rights reserved
Published by Contemporary Books, Inc.
180 North Michigan Avenue, Chicago, Illinois 60601
Manufactured in the United States of America
Library of Congress Catalog Card Number: 87-6721
International Standard Book Number: 0-8092-4775-5

Published simultaneously in Canada by Beaverbooks, Ltd.
195 Allstate Parkway, Valleywood Business Park
Markham, Ontario L3R 4T8 Canada

This book is dedicated to anyone who has ever taken a risk, stepped out on a limb, or gone to the edge—if for no other reason than the sheer and unqualified experience of it all.

CONTENTS

FOREWORD

When I first got involved in cycling as part of my training for speed skating, the sport was a small, unheard-of activity in America. Everyone interested in the sport looked to Europe as the haven of professional bicycle racers. Whenever you talked to someone about racing bicycles, it was understood that all the good riders and racers were in Europe. Bicycle racing in America was on par with archery, darts, and other esoteric recreations.

Since that time, however, (which was only in the late 1970s), tremendous changes have occurred. Bicycle racing has become a big-time sport in America, and Europeans have come to the States to race. The Coors International Bicycle Classic has become one of the premier stage races in the world. The Tour of Texas is developing into another Coors Classic. The Race Across AMerica has received national television exposure. And some of the biggest races in Europe, such as the Tour de France, the Paris–Roubaix, and the Tour of Italy, have received national television exposure stateside. And perhaps most importantly, Americans have successfully competed in major international races and come out victoriously. Greg LeMond's 1986 Tour de France victory is indicative of how far the sport has come in the last six years.

Throughout this growth period I have had the fortunate opportunity to be both a participant and an observer in cycling. The opportunity to cover the Tour de France for CBS and then participate in it the next year really gave me a feel for the beauty and toughness of this sport. Covering the Race Across AMerica for ABC allowed me to see the diversity into which this sport has grown. The next few years will see millions of Americans riding and racing their bicycles all over the country.

Michael Shermer's book is an added element to this growth. His first book, *Sport Cycling*, focused on endurance, training, and marathon cycling. This book covers a wider range of topics, such as the recent developments in technology and specialized training, as well as Shermer's expertise—sports psychology. More than the opinions of an experienced cyclist, *Cycling: Endurance and Speed* covers all the latest research into what works and what doesn't in the area of high performance. Shermer did his research homework and presents the results in a highly readable fashion.

This book is a must for anyone who wants to improve his or her ability to perform on a bicycle.

Eric Heiden

PREFACE

ON THE CUTTING EDGE

On the opening page of the first chapter of my first book, *Sport Cycling*, the incredible story of Eddy Merckx's one-hour record ride was told. Late in October 1972, Merckx rode 49.408 kilometers, or 30.23 miles, around the Mexico City velodrome, shattering the old mark and becoming the first man in history to ride farther than 30 miles in one hour. When I first entered the cycling scene in 1979 that record was considered the single greatest achievement in the history of the sport. This was not only due to the monumental effort involved in cycling for one straight hour at near anaerobic threshold, but also because of the man who broke the record. Eddy Merckx is indisputably, unarguably, incontrovertibly the greatest cyclist in the history of the sport.

Eddy Merckx won every premiere event in the sport. And he won most of these events numerous times: *five* Tours de France, *three* World Championships, *seven* Milan-San Remos, *five* Giros D'Italia, and *five* Liege–Bastogne–Lieges.

How is it possible then that a mere twelve years after

Merckx's hour record was set, on that same velodrome in Mexico City, a seemingly "second-rate" (at least compared to Merckx) professional cyclist from Italy named Francesco Moser demolished the hour record and did what Merckx claimed would never be possible—break the 50-kilometer barrier? (Moser rode 51.151 kilometers that day.)

On January 23, 1984 Moser broke Merckx's hour record because he was cycling on the cutting edge of science and technology. He used the latest developments in equipment, training, and mental preparation. He had coaches, trainers, and scientists working on every detail of his preparation. He had a disk wheel, a funny bike, a rubberized skinsuit, shoe covers, arm covers, an aero cap, aero components, aero tubing on his bike, high-altitude training, a specialized diet, and a heart-rate monitor. Moser had the physiological edge, the technological edge, and the psychological edge to beat Eddy Merckx.

In the summer of 1986, Pete Penseyres, a 43-year-old nuclear engineer from Fallbrook, California, demolished the transcontinental record in the Race Across AMerica that was set in 1985 by Jonathan Boyer, a 31-year-old seasoned European professional. How is it possible that Penseyres could cut Boyer's record down by 17 hours, as well as destroy the seemingly invincible two-time RAAM winner, Lon Haldeman, by nearly 24 hours?

Penseyres left nothing to chance. For the first time in his life he shaved his legs. He shaved his arms as well. (A .01 percent improvement in efficiency translates into real time in a nine-day bike race.) He used a disk wheel, a custom frame, and a special "table" on the handlebars that featured armrests for a more comfortable and aerodynamic ride. "On flat ground I could ride one mile per hour faster," Penseyres observed at the end of the race. The savings in time of a one-mile-per-hour improvement in more than 100 hours of flatland riding helps account for this incredible record. In addition, an aerodynamic teardrop helmet coupled with an aerodynamic skinsuit made him look and feel faster, as well as ride faster.

His bike weighed only 19 pounds. Under Penseyres's 130-pound body, the 149-pound human–bike combination made climbing hills seem effortless. (By contrast Lon Haldeman weighs 195 pounds, and coupled with a 20-pound bike, this makes for a 66-pound difference. As we shall examine in Chapter 5, even a couple of extra pounds on a long climb can add minutes to a cyclist's climbing time.)

In addition, Penseyres's diet was 80 to 90 percent liquid, consisting of 85 percent carbohydrate, 10 percent fat, 5 percent amino acids, plus the essential vitamins and minerals. This diet allows faster and more efficient digestion and less off-the-bike time for motor-home stops. Even his 90-minute sleep breaks were carefully monitored, with his wife instructed to wake him only if he was in non-REM (rapid eye movement, indicating dreaming) sleep.

And if all this wasn't enough, Penseyres added speed work to his normal megamiles endurance training. Intervals during the week, coupled with races on weekends, resulted in a 10 percent increase in speed over the same training routes used to prepare for the 1984 RAAM, which Penseyres also won in record time.

As John Kukoda of *Bicycling* magazine has noted, "Once a test of raw courage, racing across America is now a studied science." The *courage* of RAAM has now become the *science* of RAAM. To win, or for that matter even to compete successfully, you must cycle on the edge—the cutting edge of science and technology.

Excelling in a sport requires far more than just physical training. It wasn't long ago that if you wanted to be a good cyclist you merely had to go out and ride every day. Even in 1979, when I was interested in improving my cycling skills, the only advice I received was to "just go out and ride every day."

There has never been a more exciting time to be involved in the sport of cycling. Once confined to the elite, cosmopolitan road-racing circuit of northern and southern Europe, cyclists now have avenues of expression all over the world. They can compete in a variety of events, including ultramarathons, triathlons, biathlons, mountain biking, freestyling, BMX, criteriums, touring, and track racing. One is no longer restricted by the technology, training, or psychology of the past. Coaches, trainers, and athletes are aware of the need for education in the science of athletic performance.

This book is for those who want to improve themselves. The premise is twofold: (1) improvement for competitive performance, and (2) improvement for personal satisfaction. The whole point of athletics in general and cycling in particular is maintaining a lifestyle that is not only healthy but satisfying. Satisfaction comes from self-improvement, whether in competition against others or against yourself.

Cycling: Endurance and Speed will bring the reader the latest, newest, sexiest, and hottest developments in the sport of cycling. Whether they are used in races or rides, in competition or cooperation, these developments in physiology, technology, and psychology will lead to higher performance. The book is divided into three sections: The Physiological Edge, The Technological Edge, and The Psychological Edge. Within each I hope to cover far more than just my own personal opinions and self-experiments. I will give you information from actual experiments conducted on groups of cyclists under specified training and competitive conditions. I will describe the latest equipment and accessories from manufacturers. I will review the newest and most effective techniques of mental training and discipline. In other words, I hope to take the guesswork out of cycling.

For me, this book is the culmination of my two passions: science and cycling. What started out as my trained profession and vocation—science—has become almost a hobby, or avocation. And what began as my avocation and source of exercise—cycling—has become a profession. But because of developments in the science of athletics in the last decade, I have had the opportunity to combine these passions into an integrated whole—the science of cycling. I have been fortunate to observe firsthand the sport of cycling move into a new realm of achievement and performance.

In my daily life I try to strike a balance between activities of the body and activities of the mind. Achieving both mental and physical fitness is the key to an integrated and balanced lifestyle. Psychologists and physicians are now proving that such an integration is not only beneficial to your health and well-being but may actually enhance the quality and quantity of your life (see Chapter 11).

The opportunity for an individual to reach great heights is no longer limited by his not being a part of the privileged aristocracy of professional athletes. The only limitations are those you put on yourself. There is no excuse.

Michael Shermer

INTRODUCTION

Cycling has changed more in the past ten years than it did in the entire century before. There has been an explosion of new ideas on training, equipment, sports physiology, biomechanics and sports psychology. This revolution has irrevocably improved cycling equipment, concepts and performance.

Over the past 10 years the Eastern bloc countries, led by East Germany and Russia, have been producing champion cyclists by using modern science. In 1982, in response to this challenge, Ed Burke, technical director of the United States Cycling Federation, assembled a group of U.S. scientists to see what could be done to improve the U.S. team's chances in the 1984 Olympics. He asked me to organize a group to work on better equipment. By 1983 we had designed and wind-tunnel tested Kevlar disk wheels, and a complete aerodynamic bicycle and clothing system. The bicycles and clothing used by the U.S. cycling team in 1984 were technologically the most advanced in the world. Combined with modern and well-organized coaching, training, and a scientific team selection system used by the

U.S., the Americans became a leading cycle nation almost overnight, winning nine cycling medals in the 1984 Olympics.

Michael Shermer has been involved with another side of this cycling revolution—that of ultraendurance long distance racing. He is an insider who intimately knows and has contributed to the sport. This book gives a carefully researched view of what has happened, what is happening, and what will happen in cycling. This is an understandable, interesting, and useful guide for the bicycling enthusiast, written from the insider's perspective.

Chester R. Kyle, Ph.D.
Long Beach, Calif.
December 21, 1986

SPORTSPERFORMANCE

CYCLING
ENDURANCE AND SPEED

Compare body types at the 1981 Coors Classic. A lean Greg LeMond (top) leads an extremely hilly road race, well ahead of muscular Eric Heiden, following the 1980 Winter Olympics.

PART I
THE
PHYSIOLOGICAL
EDGE

"The individual rider makes or breaks himself. There is no magic formula or secret to success."
—Paul Kochli, team director
La Vie Claire, professional team

The moment that Eric Heiden won his five gold medals in the speed-skating competition at the 1980 Winter Olympics, he was an instant cycling celebrity. Why cycling? Because in ABC-TV's "Up Close and Personal," Heiden was shown in his maniacally intense training workouts, one of which included long-distance bicycle road racing. Fortunately for the promotability of the sport, Heiden loves racing bicycles and was an instant hit on the racing circuit. He was the "guest celebrity" at every race, and local television stations, which normally wouldn't touch a bicycle race with a ten-foot zoom lens, found themselves at every major climb and every hairpin corner, trying to catch a glimpse of ol' "Thunder Thighs" himself.

When I first saw Heiden compete in the 1981 Coors International Bicycle Classic in Colorado and in the Coors Devil's Cup Hill Climb outside of San Francisco, I was surprised not to find him constantly at the front of the pack. After all, Heiden was easily the most muscular mass on two wheels, and in my naivete I assumed, like most, that *muscles* mean *motion*—forward and fast.

Five years later Heiden competed in what is arguably the greatest athletic competition on the planet—the Tour de France, which is significantly longer and much more mountainous than the Coors Classic. Heiden rose to the challenge magnificently. But what I, and television viewers across the United States, observed was the newly trimmed-down and streamlined Eric Heiden. Heiden had set his goal at competing with the greatest cyclists in the world, in the penultimate contest of the sport—and did so successfully. What it took was the specialization of muscles and body to one specific task—propelling a bicycle down the highway. And Heiden, who is also studying medicine at Stanford University, took advantage of the physiological edge in training, nutrition, and biomechanics.

That information is no longer the property of a select group of athletes and coaches. It is now available to anyone and everyone interested in improving his or her competitive performance or personal satisfaction. In this first part, we will cover Basics, Training, Biomechanics, and Nutrition. Given that one is properly equipped with the latest technological developments, fine-tuning the driving mechanism of the bicycle—the human motor—is the next step.

As Lon Haldeman noted in his record-breaking performance in the 1982 Great American Bike Race, "Machines don't break records, muscles do."

A Harvard University study has shown that for every one hour of aerobic exercise, your life will be extended by two full hours. (Photo by Dave Nelson)

"One of the reasons Francesco Moser broke Eddy Merckx's hour record was that he was better prepared in his training. He was scientifically trained."

—Francesco Conconi, M.D., Coordinator,
Italian Institute of Sport Technical Committee;
Trainer of Francesco Moser for the hour record

1
TRAINING

We have probably all had the experience of witnessing a cyclist's new bike, outfitted with the latest high-tech componentry and lightweight titanium parts, only to be mounted by the rider, who is 20 to 30 pounds overweight. The gadgets are fun, and they do make a difference to the top riders, but for 99 percent of the cyclists in this country, much more can be gained through a consistent training program.

At the 1986 scientific cycling congress Dr. Francesco Conconi spoke on the "noninvasive determination of anaerobic threshold, and its value in cycling training." Translated: "How Francesco Moser broke Eddy Merckx's hour record through scientific training, and how you, too, can benefit from this type of training." Conconi suggests using a heart-rate monitor during exercise to measure the efficiency of the workout. (You may recall Francesco Moser wearing a heart-rate device on his left wrist during his training for the record attempts and actually during one of the record attempts.)

In his research Conconi studied the relationship between cycling speed and heart rate in 310 trained male cyclists. Conconi's theory is that to improve efficiency of training, one should maintain a heart rate at just below anaerobic threshold. Too far below threshold, one is wasting time and not getting the full benefit of the workout. Above the threshold there is no gain in speed, but rather a loss in efficiency as lactic acid builds up in the muscles.

Conconi's research supports his theory that a heart-rate monitor is an essential training tool. The anaerobic threshold is a fine line that must be measured scientifically, and not merely on how the cyclist "feels," especially since the pain of a good hard workout could cause one to rationalize that "overtraining" was occurring.

With Conconi's method, the $64,000 question becomes, "How do I know where my anaerobic threshold is?" The best way to determine this line, unfortunately not available to everyone, is through blood lactate measurements taken in a sports physiology laboratory. Alternatively, and admittedly a bit on the subjective side, using a heart-rate monitor one can "feel" the differences in muscular pain (indicating lactate buildup at various heart rates), as a function of increased work loads. In other words, you should gradually increase the effort on the bike, and monitor the increase in heart rate. At some point, probably above 80% of maximum heart rate, the increase in cycling speed will level off while the pain of lactate buildup continues to increase. The Dave Scott method of determining when you are just below anaerobic threshold, as noted in his book *Triathlon Training*, is that "you should be able to say at least three or four words out loud without hyperventilating."

TARGET HEART ZONE

Subtract your age from 220 to get your maximum heart rate. Then multiply this figure by .60 and .80 to get the 60% to 80% of maximum heart-rate range, also known as the *target heart zone*. For example, using my own age of 32, my maximum heart rate, and target heart zone are calculated as follows:

$$220 - 32 = 188 \times .60 \text{ and } .80 = 112 \text{ and } 150$$
$$112\text{-}150 \text{ is my target heart zone}$$

Physicians, coaches, sports physiologists, and others all recommend that those with a desire to become physically fit work out almost every day (at least four days a week) for 30 minutes within the target heart zone. This zone is the rate at which the heart is getting a good enough workout to improve and grow stronger. Less than this is almost a waste of one's time—aerobically speaking.

BENEFITS FROM TRAINING

Your heart becomes stronger and may even grow a little larger. An enlarged heart is either a diseased heart or an athlete's heart. Sports physiologist Randy Ice, who has been working with the Race Across AMerica cyclists for years, once told me about a chest X-ray he saw at a sports cardiology conference in Rome in 1978. The lecturing physician said it was the largest heart he had ever seen. All the doctors in the room agreed they had never seen anything like it—many thought it was a diseased heart. It turned out to be the heart of Eddy Merckx!

Lowers your resting pulse rate. An excellent measure of fitness level is your resting pulse rate. Highly conditioned aerobic athletes show a low resting pulse rate in the 40s and 50s. If that is your normal resting pulse rate (which should be taken at the same time every day, ideally before you get out of bed in the morning), then a sudden increase one day will indicate that recovery from the previous day's workout is not complete, and you should work out a little easier that day. The heart rate becomes a biofeedback mechanism for your training program.

Lowers your blood pressure. Well-conditioned athletes are known for their low blood pressure. This is an indication that the entire cardiovascular system is functioning well, and is not under exceptional stress.

Cleanses your arteries and veins. Daily exercise has the effect of keeping the entire cardiovascular system pumping, moving, and cleansing itself of unwanted substances, such as fat and cholesterol. Lack of exercise, together with smoking and poor dietary habits, is known to lead to the deadly disease of arteriosclerosis, or an abnormal thickening and hardening of the arterial walls.

Cleanses your pores. Anatomists and physiologists recognize the skin as man's largest organ. The best way to keep the skin clean and healthy is a daily workout that produces sweat, which removes dirt and bacteria.

Develops your lung capacity. A daily exercise program has been shown to increase vital lung capacity in all ages.

Develops your endurance. The most important factor in developing endurance is the consistency of daily workouts. It is better to work out every day for short periods of time than it is to work out once or twice a week for long periods of time.

Improves Max VO_2. Also known as "maximal oxygen consumption," this figure is the maximum amount of oxygen an individual can consume in one minute (technically, it is measured as milliliters of oxygen per weight in kilograms per minute, or ml/kg/min). It is analogous to an automobile's ability to burn oxygen and gas to produce high rpm. It is estimated that 70% to 80% of Max VO_2 is genetically determined. It is what I humorously referred to in an ABC television interview broadcast during the 1985 Race Across AMerica, when I told Jim Lampley that the only thing I could have done different was to pick better parents. However, the other 20% to 30% of Max VO_2 can be improved through training, and this can be done at any age. Barry Wolfe, a top Southern California racer, actually saw an improvement in his Max VO_2 from age 52 to 54! Age is no excuse. Joop Zoetemelk won the 1985 World Championship Professional Road Race at age 39! Pete Penseyres won the Race Across AMerica at age 43 with a Max VO_2 figure of 79.9 (the typical range for top aerobic athletes and

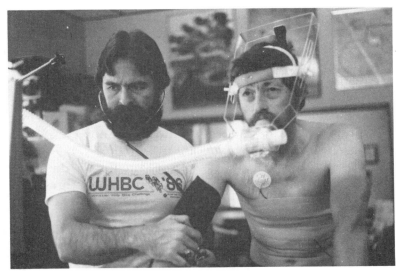

Sports physiologist Randy Ice tests RAAM champion Pete Penseyres's Max VO₂ uptake, a remarkable 79.9.

cyclists is in the 60s and low 70s). Thirty-four-year-old RAAM competitor Michael Secrest recently broke the Max VO_2 mark set by Pete Penseyres at Randy Ice's clinic with an incredible figure of 83.5! Secrest told me he is now considering challenging the hour record himself. (Typical costs for Max VO_2 testing range from $100 to $150 and the tests take about an hour to administer—a small price to pay when considering the value of knowing your physiological capacity.)

Produces endorphins. Endorphins are morphinelike substances naturally produced in the brain that reduce pain and cause a "euphoric" feeling. The production of endorphins is triggered by stress—any type of stress, especially exercise. Some sports physiologists have even speculated that "runner's high" is caused by endorphins, as is the addiction to exercise so many experience after extended periods of training. (It should also be noted that some believe the effect is entirely psychological and not tied to brain physiology.)

Randy Ice thinks that all the evidence is not yet in to

9

make a final decision on exactly where to train—above or below anaerobic threshold. He agrees that Conconi has some solid data, but points to a recent study in which three groups of runners trained below, at, or above their personal anaerobic threshold. In a three-mile running competition, the runners who had trained above anaerobic threshold were consistently faster than those who trained at or below the threshold figure. *"Where* you train," Ice observes, "will depend, in part, on *what* you are training for. The shorter the distance and the greater the speed required, the more likely it is that you should train above anaerobic threshold. When training for longer distances, it would be better to train at or below the threshold mark. But more research needs to be done in this area before we can reach any conclusions."

ADVANCED TRAINING CONCEPTS

There are a number of concepts, notions, and fallacies with regard to training that are important to understand.

IMPROVING ANAEROBIC THRESHOLD

The best way to improve anaerobic threshold is through intensity of workouts, with intensity levels of 90% to 100% of Max VO_2 spaced out into intervals during a training session. Use of a heart-rate monitor when training alone is vital, so that intervals are controlled and monitored. Cyclists have used a variety of interval methods, most commonly an on-and-off approach of either distance (perhaps one mile easy, 500 meters hard, and so on), or time intervals (perhaps structured as 30 seconds hard, three minutes easy, and so on). A couple of my training partners and I ride loops around the Rose Bowl, which is about 3.2 miles around, including a short but steep hill. On the hill side we will jam as hard as possible to the top, then coast down the other side and circle easy to the flat side of the bowl, where we will sprint from one landmark to another, approximately a quarter-mile apart, then ride easy back to the hill, jam up the hill again, and so on. We do this between five and ten times, twice a week. It is effective for quickly building your anaerobic threshold to a high level.

Riding in a pack has the same effect as interval training, except it is a more realistic duplication of racing. On one of our local Saturday rides in Southern California, a 60-mile loop, the ride will start off slowly, mostly following a downhill pattern while everyone is getting warmed up. There are a few "jams" at medium to fast speeds after about 10 miles. Then, at the 20-mile mark, on a long stretch with almost no traffic signals, the pack gets strung out as the pace picks up to about 80–90% of maximum speed. This continues for 10 miles, then at the 30-mile mark there is a short break and a chance for the rest of the group to catch up. The last 30 miles consists of short hills, sprints for city-limit signs, and recovery periods for the riders to regroup. For the final 5 miles everyone takes it easy and warms down to the end. A heart-rate monitor might prove interesting in this situation, but it is not necessary. As my friend and top triathlete George Yates says: "When the pack takes off, what are you going to do? Look down at your heart-rate monitor and say, 'Hey fellas, slow down. My heart rate is too high.' In a pack it's simple—you work or get dropped!"

WHAT IS LACTIC ACID?

There are two types of training—aerobic and anaerobic. During medium to high-medium levels of training—the aerobic level—carbohydrates and fats are used as fuel to be broken down into ATP, a process that uses oxygen and can continue for hours, and even days (as in the case of the Race Across AMerica). High levels of training—the anaerobic level—require intense activity and heavy breathing. Carbohydrates and fats are not enough to fuel the muscles at this level. There is insufficient oxygen to produce the energy, or ATP. Glycogen is the fuel used for anaerobic exercise. It breaks down into glucose, then pyruvate, and finally into lactic acid. A sufficient supply of oxygen will allow some of the lactic acid to be burned and some to be converted back to glycogen. But at 60–70% of riding intensity, lactic acid cannot be disposed of immediately. The lactic acid causes the pain you feel in an intense workout. The proteins in muscle cells can function only within a given range of acidity. Excess lactic acid shuts down the normal cellular reactions in the muscles. If the exercise and intensity continue, acute muscle fatigue and complete muscular failure will result. Tests have measured as much as 20 times the resting level of lactic acid in muscles after intense training. Anyone who has jammed as hard as possible for a long time knows that feeling of complete muscular failure—you simply cannot move your legs.

OXYGEN DEBT

Immediately after a severe workout, heaving breathing continues. The purpose of this is to repay what is called the oxygen debt. The oxygen in a muscle is quickly depleted, initiating the anaerobic energy sequence described above. Following the work, oxygen is rapidly consumed for several minutes in order to replenish the muscles' ATP energy stores. The heavy breathing also helps transport lactic acid and convert it into blood glucose or stored glycogen.

This helps explain why a rider will have to "suck wheel" at the back of the pack after he has caught up with them, because he must pay back the oxygen debt before he can once again go to the offensive at the front. Alex Steida's grand peformance to become the first North American to wear the yellow jersey in the 1986 Tour de France took such a monumental effort, that in the time trial later that day he was hurting so badly he not only lost the jersey but was almost eliminated from the entire race! The body is an elegant but simple machine—it can only take so much work, no matter how good you are.

OVERTRAINING

My first caution with regard to overtraining is that most people probably aren't, even when they think they might be. Being consistent in a rigorous training program is so difficult, most people look for any and every excuse to cut back on the intensity. However, overtraining can and does occur, with symptoms reported by U.S. Cycling Team Technical Director Dr. Ed Burke as "weight loss, decrease in strength, fatigue, elevated pulse rate, sallow skin, muscle tenderness, and poor eating and sleeping habits. Psychological symptoms are low interest in training and competition, decreased drive, slump in morale, boredom, and nervousness."

The cyclists with the greatest likelihood of suffering from overtraining are the ones who are eager to jump into the sport and reach the top overnight. They tend to be over-achievers—impulsive and impatient. Their motto may be summed up with the aerobics phrase, "no pain, no gain." I have known many a potential ultramarathon cyclist who got caught up in the glamour and glory of the depiction of the RAAM on ABC-TV's "Wide World of Sports," and immediately went out and started putting in the megamiles to the point of complete exhaustion. When I was starting my cycling career, John Howard told me, "Rome wasn't built in a day, and neither is conditioning. It takes years to become a polished and successful athlete." Coming from a cyclist who is into his third decade of bicycle racing and triathloning, this may be considered sound advice.

The main physiological problem with overtraining is a decrease in hemoglobin inside red blood cells. Hemoglobin is what carries oxygen to the muscles. Research has re-vealed a positive correlation between hemoglobin concen-tration and performance. This relationship is the basis of the concept of *blood doping*, where blood is removed well before the event (weeks), and later injected back into the body to add extra hemoglobin for greater oxygen capacity. (The advice no one will admit to giving is to inject the blood several hours before the event. After a day or two the effects are greatly diminished.) Blood doping has nothing at all to do with drugs and more resembles high-altitude training in its effects. It is now common knowledge that many members of the U.S. Cycling Team practiced this method for the 1984 Olympics, and the recent rash of successful Italian runners, including the winner of the 1986 New York Marathon, has brought this issue to light once again.

Blood tests can be given to determine the various blood

constituent levels, as an indication of proper training or overtraining. In addition to the blood tests, the resting heart rate can also be used as an indication of overtraining. A consistently high resting pulse rate probably means you need some time off the bike.

HIGH-ALTITUDE TRAINING

During the 1986 World Cycling Championships, I had the opportunity to dine with Moser's hour-record coach, Francesco Conconi, and asked him how Moser ever broke the great Eddy Merckx's record. In addition to the technological improvements—such as a disk wheel, funny bike, rubberized skinsuit, shoe covers, arm covers, aero cap, aero components, aero tubing; and physiological improvements—such as the heart-rate monitor, lactic acid testing, blood-level testing, and near-anaerobic threshold training—Conconi explained that Moser trained at high altitude and stayed in Mexico City for several weeks before the attempt. Eddy Merckx had none of these advantages.

In particular, Conconi told me that Merckx's biggest mistake was not staying in Mexico City long enough to acclimate to the altitude. It has now been shown that in order to perform at one's fullest potential at high altitude (6,500 feet or higher), it is necessary to acclimate for at least three weeks. Many of the top cyclists training for the 1986 World Championships were in Colorado a month in advance of the competition.

The effects are physiologically measurable. Sea-level air pressure is considerably higher (760 mm of mercury, compared to Mexico City at 7,400 feet and 580 mm). As a consequence, Max VO$_2$ decreases because, while the amount of oxygen at altitude is the same as at sea level, the atmospheric pressure to force it into the lungs is considerably less. Therefore, there is less oxygen available for the blood and muscles. Acclimation is the cure for this problem. At altitude the lungs, heart, and blood vessels increase in size, and there is a greater production of red blood cells and hemoglobin. The bottom line to this is that more oxygen is carried from the air to the muscles.

In 1981, a U.S. four-man time trial team trained at 12,000 feet for the national championships, which they subsequently won. Most athletes today believe in and practice high-altitude training whenever logistically possible. The evidence as to the benefits of high-altitude training, however, is mixed. Dr. Burke notes that "even in apparently well-trained athletes there has been improved performance and/or increased Max VO$_2$ upon return to sea level. In other cases there has been little or no difference. For some athletes, a slight improvement in performance upon return to sea level can be explained by a general increase in fitness." Regardless of the mixed research results, most cyclists who have had experience with this training method report that high-altitude training is effective.

Some recent evidence shows that if you cannot acclimate properly for several weeks at high altitude, it is better to go up the day before the event. When it comes to acclimation, it appears to be all or none.

THE JOY OF HILL CLIMBING

"Hills are just flats at an angle. Lon just puts it in the appropriate gear and goes."

—Ron Boi
RAAM mechanic for Lon Haldeman

From the sound of the above title you might be expecting a tome on the peak emotional experiences of climbing K–2, rappelling down Halfdome, or ascending Mount Whitney. It surely shouldn't, indeed *couldn't* be in reference to the one area of cycling that brings nearly total agreement among the normal discordant factions of the sport—the fear and loathing of climbing hills.

From commuters to tourists, from road racers to ultramarathoners, I don't think anyone actually *enjoys* climbing hills. I don't recall ever hearing anyone in the pack say, "Oh, great, a hill. I've been looking forward to this all day." Or, "All right, boys, let's see how much speed we can pick up climbing this sucker!"

Why? It's quite simple actually—hills hurt, and there are

two corollaries to go with this cycling theory: (1) Steep hills hurt more than gradual hills. (2) Long hills hurt more than short hills. We even could invoke a "law of hills": the pain and suffering of climbing hills is directly proportional to the square of the distance times the steepness of the grade!

Why is it then that some riders don't seem to hurt as much as others? Are they in better shape? Did they inherit hill-climbing genes from their parents? Or do they just have a superior mental attitude toward climbing? The answer is probably a combination of all three. Certainly no one would argue that proper conditioning is essential to improved hill climbing. If you want to be a good track racer, go race on velodromes. If you want to be a long-distance cyclist, go ride long distances. If you want to be a good hill climber, go climb hills.

But given a high level of physical conditioning, and the unchangeable, genetically determined oxygen uptake, what can you do to improve your climbing abilities? The quote by Ron Boi is a fine example of mental attitude helping to overcome a physical obstacle. Certainly Haldeman's string of victories in ultramarathon events is a testimonial to this attitude.

Is there a principle behind Boi's somewhat poetic quote, however? Yes, and it's this: when riding along a flat road at a fairly brisk pace, say 23 miles per hour, you are exerting a given amount of pressure on the pedals. When you hit a hill, the pressure remains the same as you shift to a lower gear to maintain the same cadence, even though the bike slows down. You just put it in the appropriate gear and climb. The difference is really mental. On flat ground you know you can stop pedaling and coast for a brief rest before resuming exertion. On a hill, however, if you stop pedaling, you stop.

One technique, then, is to treat hills like flat ground. Just think to yourself that if you were on flat ground you would probably be exerting yourself almost this much anyway (at least you should be, and you get a reward at the top—a flying descent with little or no pedaling!).

Another technique I use in climbing long grades of several miles or more is to break the climb down into sections and concentrate on one part at a time. In the mountains surrounding the Los Angeles basin there is a well-known 20-mile climb from the foothills to the Mount Wilson Observatory. Whenever I make this climb, I break it down into three sections: the first eight miles, at the end of which is a short downhill; the middle seven miles to Redbox, the Mount Wilson turnoff; and the final five miles up the circuitous, narrow road to the top. In addition, I break each of these sections down into smaller parts. For instance, I might just concentrate on making it to the ranger station. Once there, I focus only on the next segment to the vista turnoff, then the elevation sign, and so on.

With this technique you have to make "only" a series of short climbs—mentally. To start a 20-mile climb thinking only of the top can be psychologically defeating.

You can also alternate the way you physically climb the hill in order to overcome mental barriers. Instead of just sitting in the saddle for the entire ascent, alternate standing and sitting. You can do this by time, distance, or even pedal strokes. You might try one minute sitting, one minute standing. Or one mile sitting and one mile standing. If you don't mind counting, or if this helps distract you, alternate sitting and standing with a given number of pedal strokes.

If you like listening to music on a portable stereo, this can certainly take your mind from the pain and fatigue of climbing hills. If it is a long climb and you know it will take an hour to get to the top, just pop in an hour-long tape, and when it is over you will be there!

For competitive types who like climbing with others, a good incentive for effective hill climbing is to try to get there "The firstest with the mostest." If you are ahead, try to see how much time you can put between yourself and the others. If you aren't first, concentrate on picking off the guy in front of you. Once you get him, focus on the next cyclist, and so on until you are in the front.

There is another important factor to consider in hill

17

climbing—weight. The relationship is simple—the more weight the slower you will climb. Greg LeMond, the 1986 Tour de France winner (and the first American ever to do so), has calculated that for every extra pound of weight, whether on your bike or body, you will lose one minute of time for every thirty minutes of climbing. For instance, if you have a 24-pound bike (with 19-pound aluminum and carbon-fiber bike readily available), and are 10 pounds overweight (not unusual, according to insurance statistics), you could lose as much as 45 minutes to your lighter opponent in a 90-minute climb. Susan Notorangelo, winner of the 1985 Race Across AMerica and second in 1986, attributes Elaine Mariolle's recent RAAM victory to her ability to climb. "The decisive pass [in the RAAM] was on Yarnell Hill in Arizona," Susan told me on the final day of the race while cycling the Blue Ridge Parkway. "We were within sight of each other at the base of the climb, but by the top she was almost 30 minutes ahead." Mariolle is known for having an exceptionally low body-fat reading, particularly after a year of serious racing in preparation for the 1986 RAAM.

Your budget may prevent you from buying a new bike, but almost no one should be exempt from losing a few body pounds, which will be immediately rewarded the next time the highway takes a turn up from the flatlands.

While I can't promise that these few techniques will make hill climbing enjoyable, it certainly will give you something to think about the next time someone in the pack says: "Okay, here it comes. We'll all meet again at the bottom, right?"

QUALITY VS. QUANTITY

Training for ultramarathon races across America, Iron-man triathlons, 100-mile road races, century tours, double century rides, and even mountain biking is a matter of degree. This does not mean, however, simply riding a certain *quantity* of miles. Rather, the ability to attain excellence requires a degree of *quality* in training.

TRAINING

How to achieve success in any aspect of the sport of cycling is the most sought-after bit of information for any beginner. Everyone wants to know how to lose weight, how to increase oxygen uptake, how to strengthen the legs, how to improve hill climbing, how to develop a sprint, how to. . . . In short, everyone wants to know how to get good.

Unfortunately, the answer is not simple. There is one common thread, however, that runs through every fabric of cycling—quality training. For years I thought training for long-distance cycling was simple: more is better. I told myself: "Ride as far as you can. Day after day, accumulate as many miles as possible." Mike Secrest summarized this philosophy on ABC's "Wide World of Sports" in an interview before the 1983 Race Across AMerica: "I always train alone. I never ride with anyone else." In 1984 Secrest was reportedly covering a staggering 900–1,000 miles a week before the RAAM and Spenco 500. His performance in 1985 took a dramatic turn upward as he shaved half a day off his 1984 RAAM crossing time. Everyone was startled by this sudden increase in efficiency. Secrest said he did it by actually riding fewer miles in 1985 than in 1984. But he increased the *quality* of those miles through intense interval training, racing, and careful monitoring of his physiological functions.

My own performance in the Race Across AMerica improved considerably from 1984 to 1985. In fact, comparing the first 1,000 miles of 1985 to the original 1982 race, on the same course, I took off nearly 24 hours! Granted I did train more miles in 1985 than in previous years. In 1984 I rode 19,680 miles. In 1985 I rode 21,840 miles. That extra 2,000 miles may seem a lot until it is broken down into monthly and weekly averages:

1984 Averages	1985 Averages
Total mileage..........19,680	Total mileage..........21,840
Monthly mileage........1,640	Monthly mileage........1,820
Weekly mileage..........378	Weekly mileage..........420
Daily mileage..............54	Daily mileage..............60

Motorpacing is an excellent method for training. It forces the cyclist to maintain a high speed without allowance for rest, and in a pack teaches discipline and riding technique. In this photo U.S. track coach Roger Young leads out some of the top riders in the country at the Olympic velodrome in Los Angeles. (Photo by Dave Nelson)

Only six more miles a day pushes the yearly total up 2,000 miles. Realistically, riding an extra six miles a day will not significantly increase performance. The quality of those miles is what will make a significant difference. One would be wiser to ride hard for fewer miles than plod along at a slower pace. Riding in a pack, for instance, can make an hour of training worth several hours of easy solo riding. Riding with others always makes you ride more energetically; it creates a competitive atmosphere that makes you go faster and work harder.

CYCLOGISTICS: EVERY CYCLIST'S TRAINING LOG

It is important to chart your training progress. The accompanying graph is my own creation, using standard graph paper that can be bought at any stationery store. Simply block off the months on the horizontal axis and the miles on the vertical axis. The number of miles does not have to be recorded in 20-mile increments. It might be more psychologically encouraging if you use increments of 5 or 10 miles. After completing each training ride or race, it is reinforcing to come home and record your daily mileage. I suggest using a colored-ink pen, such as red, to really make it stand out. The graph also has a negative reinforcing effect. If you don't ride, you begin to feel guilty because you can't fill in the graph.

One of the most important aspects of riding a bicycle is the feedback on the progress you make over a period of time, Unlike other sports, such as tennis and racquetball, cycling gives you an opportunity to objectively measure your progress on a daily basis. With the advent of the bicycle computer, accurate data is now available to any cyclist at a reasonable price. Most bicycle computers measure miles traveled for the day, cumulative total miles, time elapsed, current miles per hour, average miles per hour, and revolutions per minute of the cranks. Heart-rate monitors have also become popular, and there are even some on the market that need no wire attachments—they operate by radio waves from a unit attached to the chest, to the monitor mounted on the bike.

This data is valuable to the athlete who wants to note his progress and try to improve his physical condition. But how does one record such progress?

21

Cyclogistics is for every cyclist because it isn't just the professional or serious amateur who is interested in noting his progress. Almost everyone who has ever ridden more than once is interested in knowing how he did compared to the last time he rode. It can answer such questions as: Is my monthly mileage increasing the right amount? Did I ride too many miles before the big race? Should I start my training earlier next season?

The completed cyclogistics graph below is a description of my training/racing schedule for 1985. On the horizontal axis is the year 1985 broken down into months and weeks. The months are represented to orient the reader to the time of year. It is the weeks that are important for logging the miles ridden. The blank duplication of the graph is for the reader to photocopy and use for training.

I have broken down the graph into two shades, gray and black. The gray bars are pure training weeks that do not include any races. The black bars are racing/training weeks. The Spenco 500 week, for instance, is 700 miles, since I had ridden 200 miles the days preceding the race. The 200K, 300K, 400K, and 600K signify the kilometer distances of races that the Race Across AMerica put on in 1985. The " Double Trouble" 400-mile stage race the week before the RAAM added to the training miles already accumulated that week, making it a 950-mile week. As you can see, I tapered down my training dramatically in preparation for the RAAM.

It is significant to note that a pattern can be observed, of building up to an event, cycling in the competition itself, and taking a rest period afterward. This way, in looking back over the year to assess one's progress, a quantifiable analysis becomes possible.

STARTING YOUR OWN CYCLOG

The graph sheet provided here is for logging weekly and monthly mileages. You may begin at any time of the year. If not on January 1, ignore the months and just use the numbered weeks, starting when you wish. Week 1 could begin March 21 or October 10. Your "fiscal fitness year" would then begin and end with that date. Many riders like to begin their training year with spring training in March rather than in January, when low mileage output can be discouraging to monitor. And if you are from the Eastern or Midwestern snow belt, you may not be logging any miles at all.

I have left the miles/kilometers axis blank so that you may plot mileage on it depending on the type of riding you do. Marking the squares off in increments of 10 miles will result in a total bar length of 350 miles. Twenty-mile increments nets 700 miles. If greater distances are ridden, increase the distances between squares to 50 miles at the top of the bar. Psychologically speaking, it is best to use the entire area of the graph to plot values, giving the finished product a satisfying fullness. If you typically ride 200–300 miles a week, but the graph allows room for 700 miles, you will probably develop a sense of underachievement. On the other hand, it is rewarding to fill in many squares of a bar after returning from a ride, knowing that you have trained well.

I suggest you plot the graph with a red or orange pen, as this attracts your attention and gives the psychological impression that you've trained great distances. I also recommend that you fill in the appropriate number of squares *after each ride*. Not only does it act as a reinforcer to training but it can also act as a negative reinforcer when you miss a day of riding that was not scheduled to be missed.

One trick to planning a schedule is to pencil in a mark on the bar graph before the week, to motivate you to get out there and ride to reach that goal. You can also do this in advance for the entire year, if you know your schedule well enough. Plot out the major races you want to enter, then calculate how many miles you will need to ride in preparation. Don't forget to restrict yourself to a lower mileage during the week after a big race that requires some physical or psychological recovery.

1984 TRAINING/RACING LOG

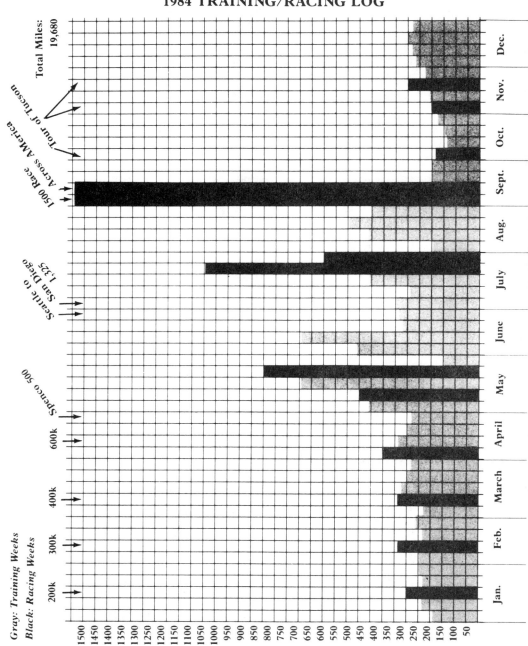

Gray: Training Weeks
Black: Racing Weeks

24

TRAINING/RACING LOG

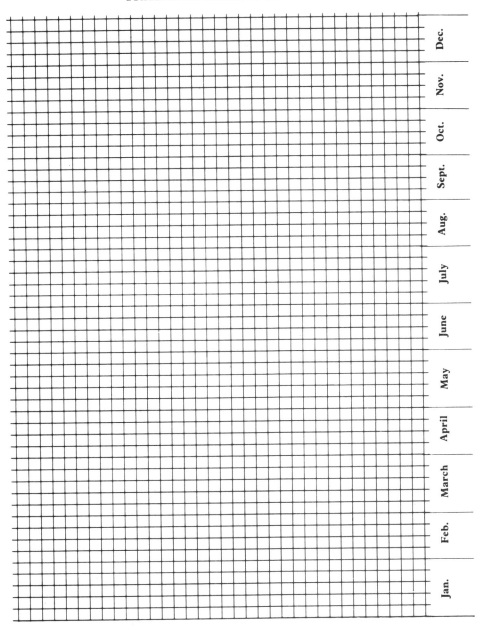

Time (Weeks per Month)

Jan. | Feb. | March | April | May | June | July | Aug. | Sept. | Oct. | Nov. | Dec.

25

Your power stroke should begin top dead center.

The ideal end of the power stroke is at dead center, where your force should be "unloaded."

"Almost all aspects of the study of the mechanics of cycling could be termed biomechanics because the human is an essential part of the mechanical system."

—Peter Cavanagh, Ph.D.
Professor of Biomechanics, Pennsylvania State University

2
BIOMECHANICS

"Pedaling in circles" has always been the description of the motion of an experienced cyclist. "Pedaling in squares" is the term used to describe the motion of a novice cyclist. Pedaling in circles is a skill developed over time and thousands of miles. Just as it sounds, it's the act of turning the pedals in a smooth, circular motion. It may seem impossible to do anything else, given that the chainring is round, which forces you to pedal in a circle, but it's not that simple. Pedaling in squares is an uneven pedal stroke in which pressure is applied to the pedals unevenly, resulting in a jerky motion. Sometimes you can see this in the motion of a bike jumping along in quick forward movements. If you ride long enough, you'll gain the "circular" status.

Dr. Peter Cavanagh discovered while testing the "elite" cyclists of the 1984 National and Olympic teams, that this issue has not been laid to rest. His findings were startling.

Pedaling may be divided into the downstroke and the upstroke. The downstroke, also known as the power stroke, begins at the top of the revolution, with the leg at the 12

Too often, the 8 o'clock position of the pedal is where most cyclists actually unload their power. This is well into the power stroke of the left leg and causes inefficiency.

o'clock position. It ends at the bottom of the revolution, with the leg at 6 o'clock. The upstroke is from 6 o'clock to 12 o'clock. The common belief that a good rider will unload the pushing force of his pedal power stroke at "bottom dead center," followed by a pulling up to "top dead center" was shown by Cavanagh to be incorrect for almost all of the National and Olympic team riders who were tested.

With sophisticated equipment attached to the pedals of each bike, Cavanagh was able to accurately measure the exact amount of force being applied by both legs at any given time in the pedal stroke. Surprisingly, almost everyone continues to push down on the pedal even when it is well on its way upward. Most of the unloading of the force occurs at approximately the 8-9 o'clock position. So in a circular pedal stroke, almost all riders are actually working *against* the opposite leg.

28

Through training and practice with the elite cyclists, using a biofeedback system, Cavanagh was able to effectively change many of the riders' style, teaching them to unload at the bottom to improve efficiency. However, if the best in the world use such a pedaling action, who is to say it isn't right? "We cannot conclude that not unloading at bottom dead center is the incorrect thing to do," Cavanagh noted "It may be what is natural for these athletes."

Since that presentation I have been working on my own pedaling style, attempting to be more aware of which position I unload the force of the stroke. It is easier to push down than to pull up. That's because of the angle of the body over the pedals, and the relatively greater strength of the quadriceps over the hamstrings (back of the legs) at that angle. Concentrate on the up portion of the stroke—it will feel awkward at first, but after a while it becomes quite comfortable.

Since most cyclists do not have access to sophisticated biofeedback machinery for pedaling (there's not exactly a big market for such a device), visualization will help you perfect this technique and translate it into reality. Picture your legs going around in circles by themselves, not in the pedals or toe straps. *Feel* the motion of going around in a circle, pushing down from the top and unloading at the bottom. It helps also to be aware of your upper-body movement. Many riders who tend to pedal in squares have much upper-body movement—swaying left to right, or jerking forward and back. Try to smooth this out and just concentrate on the muscles in the legs—they have to do the real work. (NOTE: While most of the best cyclists in the world are smooth, such notables as Alexi Grewal and the indomitable Eddy Merckx are infamous for their "attacking the bike" style of climbing.)

SADDLE HEIGHT

Saddle height has come under study recently, in light of new theories from European coaches that the saddle heights of most competitive cyclists have, in the past, been too low.

For instance, it is well known that Greg LeMond had his saddle raised by the Renault team director, Cyrille Guimard, a full five centimeters (it was done over a long period of time—the recommended way). Throughout his professional racing career, Eddy Merckx was famous for actually raising his saddle in the middle of a race, especially when a long climb was confronting him.

Early studies showed that as saddle height was raised (and muscle length increased), efficiency appeared to increase. This was attributed to the increased ability of the muscle to apply force in the elongated position (precisely the reason Merckx gave for raising his saddle, though in less technical jargon). Other studies have shown that as saddle height increased, the leg muscle turned on earlier in the pedaling cycle and stayed on longer. The 1982 Hodges study on eleven National team riders showed that the most efficient saddle height was 96 percent of leg length. Max VO_2 tests were done at varying saddle heights, and 96 percent of leg length produced the lowest oxygen consumption for the greatest work load. Interestingly, this 96 percent results in a greater saddle height than the traditional "heels-on" method, in which the rider sits in the saddle with the pedals in the 6 o'clock–12 o'clock position, and rests his heel on the lower pedal, setting the saddle at the height the leg is straight. The leg length measurement is taken from the outward bump on the hip where the leg bone inserts into the hip socket, to the center of the ankle bone. Multiply this figure by 0.96. Saddle height is measured from the center of the pedal axle in the down position to the top of the saddle, along the seat tube. Don't forget to take into account the thickness of the cleat, shoe sole, and a saddle pad, if used.

MECHANO-BIOLOGY

The other component of the formula of success, besides pedaling efficiency, is pedaling power. Biomechanics tells you how to set up your bike. Mechano-biology can tell you how to set up your body. A consistent weight-training

Measure leg in two sections.

Total and multiply by .96.

Set saddle accordingly.

program coupled with a proper cycling training program can optimize performance.

Through muscle biopsies scientists now know that there are two basic types of muscle fiber—fast-twitch and slow-twitch. Briefly, fast-twitch fibers have more power, respond quicker, and have a greater peak force than slow-twitch. Slow-twitch fibers, on the other hand, are better for endurance.

A cyclists' fast-twitch/slow-twitch ratio can be determined in a laboratory by inserting a needle three to five centimeters into the muscle and examining the resulting specimen. While your exact ratio is not the only determinant of which event you should specialize in, it can be a tool with which to understand your strengths and weaknesses.

Weight training builds muscle strength; increased muscle strength contributes to increased speed and endurance. The secret to creating a successful training program that combines weight training and cycling is to find the right balance. Weight training, for most competitive riders, is concentrated during the off-season, with half-workouts becoming the norm during race season. For racers, weight training means a competitive edge. For nonracers, it is a way to fitness—to feel and look good both on and off the bike.

HOW TO BEGIN?

Before beginning a weight program, check with your physician. Some people have physical problems that limit their exercising capacity. A doctor can advise you on what exercises you should and shouldn't do, and whether you may proceed to a full program or begin slowly and work up to a complete routine.

Next, find a gym that is equipped with modern weight machines, has a pleasant atmosphere with clean and spacious workout areas and locker rooms, and is fully staffed with knowledgeable instructors. It is best to find a gym close to your home or workplace so you're less likely to skip a session. If possible, ride your bike to and from the gym as a warm-up and warm-down exercise. Go to gyms that offer trial visits and ask members what they think. Weigh their recommendations against your observations before making a final decision.

When you're ready to begin, set aside consistent time blocks of 45 minutes to 90 minutes a day, three or four days a week. Set goals for yourself and do the exercises, allowing at least one day between workouts for recovery. Remember to take it easy at the start. An out-of-shape body takes time to return to top form. Exercising too vigorously will cause soreness and quickly sour your attitude toward weight training. Stay in tune with your body. In addition, learn to breath properly. The basic rule is to exhale when reaching the point of greatest resistance and inhale when hitting the place of least resistance. Gradually, this breathing pattern will come naturally.

Monitor your workouts by keeping a training log. Write down the repetitions, the number of sets, the number of pounds you lift, and try to describe what is happening to your body. Refer to your training log frequently; it will provide encouragement when you become discouraged about your progress.

Wear comfortable clothing. It should allow you to move without restriction. Outfits made from cotton or other natural fibers absorb perspiration and dry quickly, and are easy to care for. Don't get caught up in the yuppie fashion show at popular "social" gyms, if the clothing is not comfortable. On the other hand, if the clothes are comfortable, and looking good makes you feel good, then spend the extra few dollars for the latest threads.

There are as many different theories on weight training as there are sports that use it as a training tool. For cycling, concentrate on the lower-body muscle groups. Some cyclists also work the upper body—especially track sprinters, flat criterium racers, and triathletes.

In general, if you are going to work the upper and lower body, alternate days for each. George Yates, a consistently top-rated triathlete and one of my regular training partners, does upper-body lifting Monday, Wednesday, and

Friday and lower-body lifting Tuesday, Thursday, and Saturday, with Sunday as a rest day. Yates has a well-toned body, and his muscle groups strike a balance between strength and endurance. His endurance stems primarily from daily running, swimming, and cycling; his strength comes from weight training.

The reason for alternating days is to rest muscle groups between workouts, enabling each muscle to rebuild itself, each time stronger than before. If you don't wish to build your upper body, the off-days can be used for hard workouts on the bike. For most competitive cyclists who do not participate in triathlons or track racing, extra upper-body muscle is just extra weight to carry up hills. Whatever arm strength is needed for out-of-the-saddle climbing can easily be developed by just riding.

WARM UP FIRST

The first step in anyone's weight routine should be a warm-up. There is no surer way to injure yourself than to walk in cold and begin lifting weights without adequate warm-up. Warm-up entails two processes. The first is elevating the heart rate through aerobic exercise, the second is stretching. Stretching prepares the muscles for strenuous work and heavy loads. Riding to the gym will solve the first problem.

An aerobic warm-up is best attained by running, cycling, or stair climbing. Any of these activities conducted for 10 to 15 minutes before lifting weights will enrich the muscles with the blood and nutrients they will need for the routine. At many health clubs, there are both stationary bikes and stair-climbing devices for a warm-up. The warm-up should be undertaken at a medium pace.

THE WELL-PLANNED WORKOUT

Your workout plan should be designed by someone who knows and understands cycling and the specific muscle groups you want to work on.

You don't need to overdo the number of repetitions at the weight station; it's best to do two or three sets of each exercise. Complete the full routine, one set at each station, then repeat. Some people prefer to do all their sets at a station before moving on. Either way is acceptable, though the former may provide more variety and decrease boredom.

The amount of weight you use should be determined by an expert working at the gym. It is better to start with too little weight than too much. Once you have established your starting weight, begin to increase it slowly and systematically as the weeks and months go by. If you suffer pain and stress in joints, decrease the amount or type of exercise rather than try to tough it out by forcing the motion. An injury can delay your weight-training program for a long time.

There may be many exercises besides those represented here that are applicable to cyclists and triathletes. The value of each should be determined by the effect it has on your overall performance on the bicycle.

Dips. Dips are the most hated exercise in the gym—especially if you aren't accustomed to doing them properly. Grip the two posts and lower yourself as far as possible, creating at least a 90-degree bend in your arm. This builds tremendous strength in the shoulders and triceps. Do as many as possible at first, but top out at 20 a set, three sets a day.

Warm up properly by stretching. Stretch your left calf and hamstring, then your right calf and hamstring, then both together (as well as the quads) by touching your toes. Stretch your quads by pulling your foot back and up toward your buttocks.

A second set of stretches to be done on the floor: Reach for your toes to stretch the hamstrings. Pull your feet as far toward your body as possible to stretch your quads and groin muscles. Finally, with your back flat on the ground and your left leg stretched out, cross your right leg over and pull upward and toward the ground. This stretches many muscle groups, including and especially your hip area. Then switch legs and repeat the stretch.

37

After the stretching warm-up, 10 to 15 minutes on a stationary bike will get your muscles working, your heart pumping, and your blood flowing. This prepares your body for the weight workout to follow. I always finish the workout session with 10 to 15 minutes on the bike to loosen the muscles, warm down the body, and remind my legs of their real job—cycling.

The Lunge. With a manageable weight in each hand (about 25 to 35 pounds), "lunge" forward with each leg—left, right, then left again. When beginning, it is good to "walk" through the lunges slowly. As you build your strength and balance, increase the speed to the point where each lunge takes only about a second. Repeat 25 lunges for each leg for a total of 50 each set, three sets a day.

This exercise was created by Jonathan Boyer to develop upper-body strength for out-of-the-saddle climbing. Hold a manageable weight of 20 to 25 pounds in each hand. Then alternate thrusting the weights forward—left, right, then left again, over and over. Picture yourself on the bike, out of the saddle, and pulling the handlebars back and forth. Repeat the motion 100 times three times a day.

Lat Pulls. Lat pulls are excellent for building strength in the lats and shoulders. Do 15 repetitions, three sets a day.

Michael Coles demonstrates an exercise to build strength in the biceps, triceps, and lats. Start with 20 to 30 pounds and alternate pressing each weight, about 25 times total, two sets a day.

Coles works on his deltoids (the back of the upper arm) by lifting both weights simultaneously from the down position parallel to the legs, to the up position parallel to the ground. Repeat 10 times each, two sets a day.

Back Stretches. Using a solid stick or bar, these two stretches are an excellent way to relieve muscle tension in the middle of a workout session. I do 25 of each, alternating left and right to count as one.

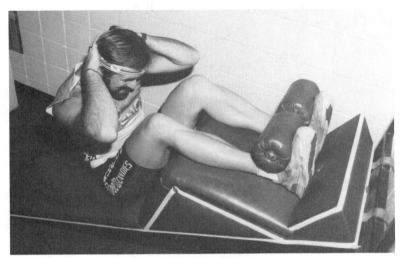

Sit-ups. I do a set of 25 sit-ups after every other weight set. By the end of the workout I've done several hundred sit-ups, strengthening my abdomen muscles and adding support to my lower back area.

This is an excellent exercise for strengthening your lower back.

Leg press. Leg presses build the quadriceps. Use an amount of weight that will only allow you to do about 25 repetitions before fatigue and pain cause muscle failure.

Leg Curls. On the leg-curl machine lie flat on your stomach and curl the weights up toward your buttocks. This is a difficult exercise and can strain the hamstring muscles, for which it is an ideal exercise to build strength. I recommend starting with a small weight, 30 to 40 pounds, and doing 25 repetitions, three sets a day.

Leg Pulls. Hook a weight belt to your left ankle and harness it to a weight machine. Holding onto a firmly planted object in front of you, pull your left leg as far forward as possible, lifting your knee high and toward your chest. Do three sets of 25 a day on each leg.

Squats. Squats are the most common weight exercise for building strength in the legs for sprinting in track and criterium races. Coles, a weight lifter and top cyclist from Atlanta, demonstrates the proper position from which to begin the squat. Repeat the squat 10 times, three sets a day.

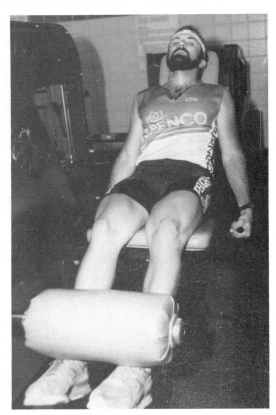

Leg Extension. Excellent for building strength in the quadriceps, this exercise should be done in three sets each day, about 25 in each set.

Finger Push-ups. I do three sets of 25 a day. This type of push-up not only builds strength in the upper chest and shoulders but in the hands and wrists as well.

Backswing. When the workout is over, with either weights or on the bike, a relaxing upside-down hang will stretch out your spinal vertebrae and force blood from your legs to your brain, so that you won't suffer from the mental disorder I call "train brain," in which memory and other vital mental functions seem to break down.

Pete Penseyres sports the latest in technology and style: teardrop helmet, lycra skin-tight clothing, suspension-wear glasses (no frame), disk wheel, shaved arms (and legs, of course), and an armrest device that makes riding in a hunched over/flat-back position possible. (Photo by Dave Nelson)

*"The single biggest reason people quit riding their bikes is
pain. Everyone wants to be comfortable on a bike."*

—Dr. Wayman Spence
Founder, Spenco Medical Corporation

3
COMFORT

On a recent training ride with the local racing club in my
neighborhood (which, when you live in Southern California, typically means the presence of national team members
such as Thurlow Rogers), several of us were discussing the
most painful athletic experiences of our lives. I brought up
the subject when we passed the turnoff for a mountain road
that was the start/finish of a nine-mile mountain running
road race I had participated in several months previously.
This was one of the most painful memories of athletic
competition for me—running four and a half miles straight
up the side of a mountain (approximately a 25 percent
grade), and four and a half miles back down. I was
cramping, foot faulting, and hunched over in pain—but I
wasn't alone. Almost everyone was in this state of misery,
and I finished fairly high up at 62d out of more than 350
participants.

Barry Wolfe, one of the local gurus and "senior states-
man" of our local cycling group, commented that it was

this sort of pain and discomfort seen on the faces of runners that makes cycling so appealing to him. "Cycling is just so good for your body," Wolfe said as we breathed heavily up the long climb. "Even when you're hurting it's not the same kind of pain that runners feel. Your body is comfortable on a bicycle. It belongs on a bike. I could ride for the rest of my life."

Barry's last comment sums up for me what the meaning of riding bicycles is—an exercise for life, and a lifestyle of fitness. But for cycling to be truly enjoyable, you must be comfortable on the bike. Once the bicycle is properly set up, then you're on your way.

COMFORT IS KEY

In both the 1984 and 1985 versions of the longest single-day bicycle race in the world, the Spenco 500, the turna-round halfway point in the southern part of the rolling hills of Texas was the key to the race. Whoever was leading after that point had the inside track to the kudos and the $10,000. In 1985 it was Steve Speaks and Shelby Hayden-Clifton, and in 1986 it was Tom Prehn and Betsy King. In both instances, the halfway leaders went on to win the race. That turnaround point was the town of Comfort. Comfort held the key to winning the Spenco 500, in more ways than one. Whether you're racing or riding, whether you're going 500 miles, 50 miles, or just 5 miles, comfort is the key to enjoying your trip.

Many major body areas—the feet, knees, rear, hands, neck, arms, and back—are susceptible to discomfort while riding. There may be others, of course, but these spots are typically troublesome for cyclists. One of the purposes of the Spenco 500 race was to use the event as a testing ground for Spenco's sports medicine products for cyclists. Many of the top riders from the United States and Europe were using Spenco gloves, saddle pads, handlebar grips, and insoles. Spenco then took the information these riders provided them on the effectiveness of the products and incorporated it into their product design.

COMFORT

FEET

Two typical problems with the feet are arch pain and "hot foot." Arch problems probably stem from wearing tennis shoes instead of cycling shoes. Proper cycling shoes, whether cleated racing shoes or uncleated touring shoes, have stiff soles to support the arch and provide pedaling efficiency. You don't have to push through a thick cushion, as with a tennis shoe. For racing, cleated shoes are a must because they hold the foot on the pedal and allow you to pull up as well as push down. This is much more efficient and can help relieve some of the pressure on the arch. Some people have arch-support problems anyway, in which case an orthotic may help. The advantage of touring shoes is that you can walk normally in them when you aren't cycling. Cleats make walking more difficult.

"Hot foot" may be caused by riding in the heat, by shoes that are too tight, or by feet not built to push a hard sole. For some, the solution is to use a comfortable touring shoe with a semisoft sole, such as the Bata Biker, or any of Avocet's designs. Pete Penseyres won both the 1984 and 1986 RAAM with Avocet touring shoes. For those who wish to continue using a cleated shoe, an insole can be inserted to provide some cushion while not detracting from efficiency.

One final problem of the feet is swelling. If you have this problem, you can use shoes that are a half-size larger, or slit the sides of your regular shoes with a razor blade, where the little toe presses against the shoe.

KNEES

The angle at which your foot rests on the pedal can cause knee problems. If the foot is turned in or out too much, it may cause the knee to follow through its circular motion at an odd angle and put stress on the tendons on either side of the kneecap. Most cleated shoes have adjustable cleats. Try different angles until you find the most comfortable position, then lock it down.

Knee problems related to poor seat position can be easily corrected. As a general rule, if there is pain behind the knee, the seat is probably too high. If the pain is on top or

51

on the side of the knee, the seat is probably too low. To set your seat height correctly, sit on the seat with both feet on the pedals. You will need someone to hold the bike for you or lean against a wall. With the pedals in the 6 o'clock and 12 o'clock positions (straight up and down), there should be approximately a 10-to-15-degree bend in the knee of the straighter leg. Never should your leg be perfectly straight. Take the bike for a ride. When you pedal, your hips should not be rocking back and forth. If they do, it means you are reaching for the pedals and the seat should be lowered.

If you use the popular new Look safety pedal system, where you merely step into the pedal, which locks onto the cleat (like a ski binding), your saddle should be raised slightly because the cleat adds maybe one-third to one-half inch to your height. This new system is far superior to the traditional toe strap/slotted-cleat system used in the past. There is no longer a toe strap to dig into your instep, and it is quite impossible to come out of the pedal, even on a hard climb. Yet, a simple twist of the heel, left or right, will pull the foot right out when you desire to stop. It is likely that within a few years no serious rider will be using toe straps any longer.

Regardless of your current seat height, raise or lower the seat gradually over a period of about two weeks in order to allow your knees to adjust to the new torque and angle.

Knee problems may also be caused by incorrect saddle position. Your saddle can be adjusted forward and backward as well as up and down, and there is a general rule for that, too. Sit on the bike with your feet in the pedals again, and rotate the pedals to the 3 o'clock and 9 o'clock positions, parallel to the ground. Take a plumb line or a piece of string with a nut or bolt tied to the end, and hold the string on the side of the forward leg, positioned at the middle of the kneecap. Let it drop straight down somewhere near the axle of the pedal. Ideally, the string should fall directly through the middle of the pedal axle. If it falls behind the axle, move your seat forward. If it hangs in front of the axle, move your seat back. The angle at which the knee makes the pedal revolution can affect efficiency and comfort. For accuracy and consistency in fitting a bike to your body, a device called the Fit Kit is designed specifically for sizing and positioning on a bike. Most quality racing shops carry the Fit Kit, and I highly recommend it for both the novice and experienced rider. It is quite expensive, so you probably wouldn't want to buy one unless you plan to use it for a lot of people.

BUTTOCKS

Do not be deceived by any bike expert on the subject of the buttocks. No one is exempt from the possibility of saddle sores. Obviously, the more you ride, the more you will become accustomed to sitting on the saddle. Your skin will develop a toughness that will help protect it. Of course, the more you ride, the greater the likelihood you'll be exposed to conditions that could trigger the development of saddle sores. Precautions must be taken.

The saddle itself can help prevent soreness. There are many types on the market—leather, plastic, synthetic, and combinations of leather, plastic, and padding. Regardless of what type you select, make sure you break it in and adjust to it before you switch. Leather saddles usually need to be

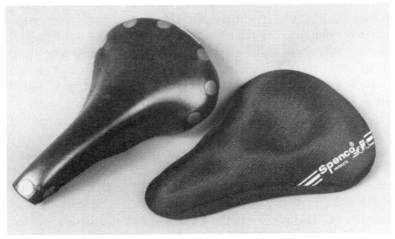

The hard leather surface of a saddle, such as the Brooks Professional shown here, can be made more comfortable with a padded saddle cover.

softened and broken in, which takes time and many miles of riding. The process can be accelerated by soaking the saddle in a big baggie filled with a liquid leather softener available at most equestrian saddle shops. RAAM finisher Susan Notorangelo has always used a Brooks leather saddle, as have I, and she feels that it is excellent once your rear is used to it and it forms to your shape.

A simpler solution is a good-quality saddle pad like the Spenco Saddle Pad. While there are many on the market, what you should look for is a pad that distributes road vibrations evenly throughout the seat and away from the pressure points in your rear. Many seat covers and pads, such as those made of sheepskin, may seem comfortable at first, but when broken in, the material will not retain its original shape. Using feedback from the racers in the Spenco 500, Spenco developed an extremely light and thin racing saddle pad that is ideal for someone who doesn't have a lot of seat problems but wants to be a bit more comfortable.

Cycling shorts can also contribute to comfort. They are generally better than running or tennis shorts because they are made specifically for the pedaling motion and will not "creep" up on you and cause chafing as other shorts might. Also, your cycling shorts should be washed after each wearing because the bacteria that accumulate from dirt and sweat can cause saddle sores to develop much sooner than need be. In the Race Across AMerica and other long-distance rides I always change my shorts daily and wash thoroughly to prevent sores from starting.

For many women I ride with, especially on the tandem, it isn't just their rear that bothers them. The "lower front" area (as my wife calls it), or the genital area, becomes sore and chafed. The saddle pad solution is effective, but if that doesn't work, try tilting the saddle back so that the nose of the seat is higher than the back. This may not seem logical at first, but it has the effect of forcing you to sit back on the two bones in your rear, instead of leaning forward on the lower front area.

A good pair of padded cycling gloves can mean the difference between comfort and misery when riding a bike.

HANDS

As with knee problems, positioning on the bike can help eliminate hand problems. The tilt of your saddle can determine the amount of pressure your hands will exert on the handlebars.

The most common hand problem is numbness of the fingers, caused by pressure on the superficial nerve that lies just under the skin of the palms. This numbness is called palmar palsy, and it can be annoying or even end a cyclist's career if the condition grows serious.

As a rule, the angle of the seat should be parallel to the top tube. If you are having hand problems, tilt the nose of the saddle slightly upward. This will force you to sit farther back on the seat, relieving some of the pressure on the hands. Try this several times at different angles until you get a comfortable balance in pressure. However, if the saddle nose is tilted too high, this can cause extra pressure in the groin area, possibly causing numbness and thus defeating your original purpose. For any discomfort prob-

55

lem, change the position of the seat until it feels right, making sure to give it enough time for an honest test.

I also strongly recommend a good pair of cycling gloves. The leather covering will help prevent chafing and blisters. If they are padded properly, gloves can protect the superficial nerve in the palm and therefore prevent numbness. Like the seat pad, the glove padding should distribute road vibration evenly across the glove surface and away from the pressure point on the palm. The elastomer found in the Spenco gloves and saddle pads does exactly that. And once again in response to the racers, Spenco now has its "TL 500" glove that is not quite as bulky; the back is also much more comfortable, as it is terry cloth/lycra instead of the mesh weave.

It is good practice to shift the hands around the bars frequently so that pressure can't build up at any one point. You can ride with your hands on top of the bars, on the brake hoods, in the curve of the drops, or on the bottom of the drops. Shifting every 30 seconds or so will help relieve pressure.

NECK

The handlebar stem length also requires adjustment on the bike. This can greatly affect the angle of your neck. Place yourself on the bike with both feet in the pedals and your hands on the drops and look straight down toward the axle of the front wheel. You should not be able to see it; it should be concealed by the handlebars. If the axle is in front of the handlebars, you need a longer stem. If the axle is behind the handlebars, you need a shorter stem. For women with a short torso, for whom even the shortest of alloy stems is too long, I suggest the short steel stem found on many 3-speed bikes. Specialized has a 6-centimeter stem, as does TTT and SR; the latter also offers a 5-centimeter stem. It is advisable to get a new stem rather than push your saddle too far forward, thus changing the angle at which your knee is positioned over the pedal axle, as discussed previously.

COMFORT

On that same subject, small women may want narrower handlebars, made by some of the Japanese bike companies. They come as narrow as 36 centimeters, which should put your arms even with your shoulders if you have a petite body structure. (For further information on positioning for women, as well as many other important topics on women's cycling not covered in this book, I suggest Elaine Mariolle's new book, *The Woman Cyclist,* coauthored by me and published by Contemporary Books.)

A new stem may not be necessary, however. First try adjusting your seat backward or forward until the front axle disappears. But keep in mind the plumb experiment performed earlier for proper knee positioning.

Neck stiffness can be relieved when riding by exercising to loosen the muscles. When stopped at a signal, let your head drop to your chest, then rotate it, and you will feel the tension disappear. Repeat this in the opposite direction. You might also try rubbing your neck with your hands to relieve a little tension. If you have serious problems with your neck, however, consult a doctor or chiropractor for a professional opinion.

ARMS

The main problem related to the arms is fatigue. Fatigue in this case also radiates into the shoulders and upper back. The cause of this problem is twofold: incorrect positioning on the bike and lack of strength.

As with other areas of the body, the ability of your torso to support itself while riding can be helped or hindered by your position. If the stem is too long, you are stretched out too far, making it uncomfortable for your arms and forcing you to lock your elbows. Locked elbows result in the vibration from the highway traveling directly through the bike into your hands and arms, and finally into the shoulders and back, which must absorb the shock.

If the stem is too short, it forces the body into an upright position that is more suited to a 3-speed touring bike than to a 10-speed racer. This position causes you to bunch up

57

your shoulders and draw your arms in toward your body, which can lead to tension and tightness in the upper back, shoulders, and arms.

Correct stem length, as determined by the process described in the "Neck" section, should benefit you. The correct position for the arms requires them to bend anywhere from 45 to 90 degrees at the elbow. This makes the elbow a "shock absorber" for the rest of the body. Your arms should be relaxed, not stiff and tight. The bicycle moves forward by the pedaling action of your legs, not by gripping the handlebars with tensed arms. As the great Eddy Merckx once responded to a reporter who commented on the small size of his arms, "It doesn't take much strength to steer a bike!"

In addition to being bent at the elbows, the arms should be parallel to the top tube of the bike. They should not bow out from the body, for this is not only more tiresome but also less efficient aerodynamically, since the arms can catch wind and slow you down. This position may seem awkward at first if you are not accustomed to it, but a few weeks of practice should remedy arm fatigue.

Just as some women may need narrower handlebars, they may also need shorter-reach brake levers. Shimano's Dura Ace AX and 600 AX are adjustable, and Dia-Compe and Weinmann manufacture "junior" levers that are ideal for small hands.

Arm fatigue can also be caused by lack of strength. Many cyclists have seriously unbalanced bodies, with huge, magnificent legs and skinny, weak arms. Though Merckx was essentially correct in his observation, a certain amount of arm strength is valuable when climbing hills by standing out of the saddle and when sprinting, touring, or riding long distances. Many women complain of a weakness in the upper body that cycling doesn't help. In that case, weightlifting and sports such as swimming can help build strength that may be called upon in cycling. Chapter 2, on biomechanics, described some upper-body exercises that can strengthen the torso for cycling.

I have found that swimming helps a great deal with upper-body development while at the same time providing aerobic training. Using the four basic swimming strokes—freestyle, backstroke, breaststroke, and butterfly—you can build considerable strength and force your lungs to work. Swimming can also be great novelty for those who ride so much that cycling occasionally becomes a chore. Many a cyclist became a triathlete through cross-training.

BACK

Much of the advice concerning the arms and shoulders applies to the back. In particular, stem length and tension in the upper back and shoulders are related to back problems. The lower back, however, involves different muscles. If you have lower-back problems related to cycling, the solution may not be difficult. On the other hand, if like most people with back problems your lower-back pain exists regardless of activities on the bike, the prognosis may not be as optimistic or as simple.

I can sympathize with anyone suffering from back pain. It can range from a dull, irritating ache to a crippling pain that interferes with normal daily activities. For three years of my life I was plagued by what began as a sharp, intermittent pain in the lower left side of my back, and progressed to a constant dull ache covering my entire lower back. It finally became a crippling agony that forced me to consume 10 to 20 painkilling tablets a day. Trips to new physicians, experts in the field of spinal disorders, failed to cure the problem. I went from one doctor to the next, trying over a dozen in three years. The diagnoses ranged from scoliosis and arthritis to blood disorders and a spinal tumor. The latter theory turned out to be the correct diagnosis. The prognosis ranged from 100 percent recovery to a life without movement, and even the possibility of death. One doctor told me to give up athletics and develop my mind. Another had me wear a body cast that held me rigid from neck to waist for a full year. Since the only sport I could participate in was archery, I had fun startling the coach by having a friend shoot arrows at my chest. The arrows bounced harmlessly off the cast, which was hidden by my shirt!

The solution to my back problem was surgery to remove the previously unseen tumor. It had, over the course of three years, grown large enough to be detected by special X-ray techniques. Its removal was also the cure for the pain.

Not everyone is as lucky as I was. My fellow ultramarathon cycling competitor and friend John Marino has suffered back pain occasionally ever since a weightlifting accident terminated his career as a professional baseball player. The only sport that allowed him to compete without excruciating pain was cycling. Though he has tried chiropractors, fasting, hanging upside down, massage, and many other therapies, he still occasionally suffers from the pain.

I won't pretend that by simply changing your stem length or seat height you can make your pain disappear. The lower back, in particular, doesn't respond readily to such simple cures. Marino has tried hundreds of different combinations of positions on the bike, some of which work better than others, but none of which completely solves the problem.

For my back, even though I no longer have pain, I hang upside down every day from a device called the Backswing. This helps stretch out the spinal column and really feels good after a long day scrunched up on the bike. When you swing upside down you can feel and hear the joints cracking—the tension just seems to pour out.

The Fit Kit discussed earlier is highly recommended for proper positioning that may eliminate some back problems. The ideal solution may be to have a bike custom-made for your body. Expert frame builders will consider inseam length, arm length, torso length, overall height and weight, and style of riding when they design your frame. Even the frame geometry, or the angles of the tubing, can make a difference in the comfort of the bike. For small-framed women especially, a custom bike may be the answer to all positioning problems.

COMFORT

Finally, with all the rules and generalizations regarding positioning on a bicycle for comfort, only you can decide on the most comfortable position for your body. All bodies are different, and no single position will be correct for all people. You can use these guidelines to help, but ultimately your comfort can be determined only by you, the cyclist.

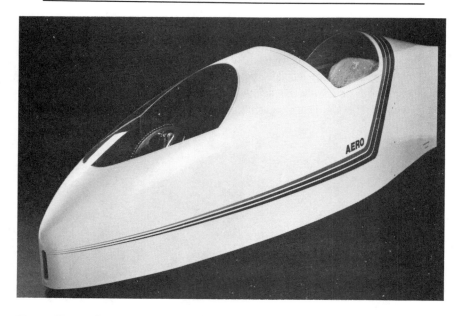

Two recent designs that have attempted world records at the International Human-Powered Speed Championships. (Photo courtesy of Eric Conrad)

"Aside from the influence of training, no other factor seems to have as great an impact on performance as the dietary habits of the cyclist."

—David Costill, Ph.D.
Director, Human Performance Laboratory,
Ball State University

4 *NUTRITION*

Nutrition is one of the *most* important and *least* understood (or perhaps most confusing) areas involved in sports performance. Eating is an activity we engage in three or more times every day, yet we rarely consider the consequences of what has just passed our lips and entered our biological machine. The analogies of the body to a machine are obvious. And like any machine, the body needs to be refueled. The two main questions are: with what, and how much?

The famous bestseller *Eat to Win* by Dr. Robert Haas (and endorsed by Martina Navratilova) recommends this "peak performance" ration of foods:

Complex carbohydrates (starches)	60–80%
Simple carbohydrates (sweets)	5–10%
Proteins (animal and vegetable)	10–15%
Fats (animal and vegetable)	5–20%

Ed Burke notes in *The Two-Wheeled Athlete*: "A cyclist's daily diet is normally composed of 45% carbohydrates, 30%–40% fat and 15%–20% protein." U.S. National team coach Eddy B.'s recommended breakdown is:

Carbohydrates	60%
Proteins	15%
Fats	25%

Pete Penseyres used a diet of 90% liquid fuel during his 1986 Race Across AMerica victory, a diet that consisted of the following percentages:

Carbohydrates	85%
Proteins	5%
Fats	10%

My preference, which has evolved over many years of experimentation (and not necessarily just for ultraendurance cycling) is:

Carbohydrates	70%
Proteins	20%
Fats	10%

My rule of thumb is to maximize carbohydrates, optimize proteins, and minimize fats. Unsaturated fats, such as vegetable oil, are better than saturated fats, such as those that come from animals (butter, milk, etc.). Saturated fats have been linked to arteriosclerosis and heart disease. On the other hand, Derk Pearson and Sandy Shaw, authors of the controversial book *Life Extension*, cite evidence that unsaturated fats have been linked to cancer because they release so-called free radicals in digestion. As Pearson notes, it all depends on how you want to go!

The standard American diet consists of these incredible proportions:

Carbohydrates	40%
Proteins	15%
Fats	45%

Anthropologists quip that twentieth century man lives like a Homo sapiens but eats like a Neanderthal. In other words, the typical American diet might contain a huge prime-rib steak; but instead of following this with several days of foodless hunting and gathering in the jungle, modern man goes to his air-conditioned office to become a couch potato. The ideal diet is somewhere near the athletic figures, whether you are a full-time athlete or not. The sort of foods that make up the above categories are most commonly the following:

Carbohydrates:

- Cereals
- Fruits (fresh, dry, or in juice form)
- Vegetables (raw or steamed)
- Rice
- Potatoes
- Grains (breads, pancakes)

Proteins:

- Dairy Products (milk, cheese, yogurt, cottage cheese)
- Meats (poultry, fish, shellfish, veal, beef, duck, pork, lamb)
- Legumes (beans, peas, lentils)
- Nuts and Seeds

Fats:

- Oil (vegetable, peanut)
- Butter
- Margarine
- Mayonnaise
- Ice Cream

CARBOHYDRATES

To determine the correct amounts of the right type of foods, you must understand the physiology of the cyclist. The primary fuel source for most cyclists is carbohydrates.

But they are not the only source. The metabolism of fats can also be a vital source of energy. The shorter the race, the more dependent the cyclist is on carbohydrates. The longer the race, the more the cyclist will utilize fats for fuel. Although fat stores are greater than carbohydrates (they contain more energy per gram), they require more oxygen to metabolize, which is desperately needed in shorter and faster events. In long-distance road races and ultramarathon events, oxygen consumption is reduced, and fat stores can be tapped. Dr. Ed Burke reports that the metabolism of carbohydrates is 7% to 8% more efficient than that of fat during heavy work loads.

Interestingly, the more and longer you train, the greater your body's ability to metabolize fats efficiently. It has been shown that in rides of four to five hours and more, you are training your body to switch from carbohydrates to fat as the primary energy source. Dr. Burke notes: "In a road race the highly trained cyclist who operates at 80 to 85 percent of his Max VO_2 while accumulating very little lactic acid can obtain a relatively great amount of energy from fat stores. On the other hand, a less well-conditioned rider can complete the first 75 percent of the race with some ease, but then experiences the 'bonk' in the final miles."

Penseyres's performance with his top-heavy carbohydrate diet confirms the research findings. And carbohydrate loading among endurance (but not necessarily ultramarathon) athletes has become legendary. In marathons and road races the level of work intensity is high, with a corresponding demand for carbohydrate fuel. Prolonged intense work is known to lead to a significant loss of glycogen, and thus glucose levels in the blood. "Carbo loading" has the effect of elevating the muscles' stores of glycogen, the primary fuel used in the ATP energy process. The experts have designed (after much experimentation) a basic one-week, before-the-event program:

- Days 1–3: low carbohydrates, high proteins and fats.
- Days 4–7: high carbohydrates, low proteins and fats.

Days 6 and 7 in particular demand almost a 100% loading of carbohydrates, and have led to such prerace events as "pasta parties." While this has proved to be quite effective, physicians do not recommend this routine on a weekly basis. It is suggested that you peak for several events throughout the year, with several months between events.

PROTEINS

Little of the energy used by a cyclist comes from protein sources, and may amount to less than 4%. However, protein is essential in the construction of enzymes, the catalysts involved in all cellular metabolic processes, as well as the structural components of cells—muscle cells included. In other words, there are two types of proteins: (1) structural proteins (the material of cells), and (2) enzymes (the function of cells). Proteins themselves are made of amino acids, which have been called the building blocks of life. There are 20 amino acids in nature, 19 of which are contained in various foods. They are divided into two groups: essential and nonessential. Essential amino acids are necessary for growth and development, and come from foods. Nonessential amino acids are produced by the body.

Proteins are divided into complete and incomplete. Complete proteins contain all the essential amino acids, while incomplete proteins are missing one or more amino acids. Complete proteins are included in the list of proteins near the beginning of this chapter. Incomplete proteins include grains, vegetables, and nuts. An omnivorous diet containing both animal and plant foods will provide all essential amino acids. Vegetarians must combine incomplete proteins in order to provide all the essential amino acids. For protein synthesis to occur, all the essential amino acids must be present. The RDA (Recommended Daily Allowance) figure for protein, for a 150-pound individual, is 54 grams a day. This is easily met by a diet containing the protein percentages of any of the suggested diets already discussed, including Penseyres's 5% protein (providing it is taken through his liquid formula, which includes all the essential amino acids).

FATS

If fats can be excellent sources of energy, then what type of fats should you eat? If you're aiming for a 5–15% daily intake of fat, then one tablespoon of olive oil, vegetable oil (safflower, corn, or sesame), margarine, or mayonnaise is recommended a day. The American Heart Association suggests eating the "friendly" fats found in salmon and mackerel, and the "essential" fats that occur in such foods as oatmeal, corn, and brown rice. The American diet and most American restaurant foods are so rich in fat that even if you think you are avoiding fats altogether you are probably getting more than the daily allotment.

It has been shown quite conclusively, and powerfully, that being overweight (almost always from too much fat—the Eric Heiden example in the preface to this section of having too much muscle is the exception), directly impedes performance. The fact that the two winners of the 1986 RAAM, Elaine Mariolle and Pete Penseyres, were the lowest in body fat for their respective divisions, is no coincidence

THE LATEST FINDINGS

David Costill, the director of the Human Performance Laboratory at Ball State University, reported at the 1986 scientific cycling congress that there are many "trendy" fads that come and go, but most of these have no basis in fact. For instance, there is absolutely no evidence that megavitamin and megamineral supplements improve performance. For example, in six hours of continuous exercise you lose only one percent of the minerals in your body, which are easily replaced by the normal intake of food during that session.

Costill feels that the key area of research is in the depletion of carbohydrate fuel, in the form of muscle glycogen, from the muscle during exercise. The goal is the replacement of that fuel. He reported that a trained athlete stores approximately twice the amount of muscle glycogen a normal person does. But, of course, the training schedules most professional athletes are on drain the glycogen much faster—thus the need for proper nutrition.

Costill traced the sequence of energy transfer as follows: *food—glycogen—glucose—blood—muscle*. When a muscle can't get the glucose it needs from the blood, it uses its own store of glycogen faster. This leads to the conclusion that glucose must be added to the bloodstream at a steady rate throughout the exercise session. Costill's research has shown that the ideal is to eat a light carbohydrate meal before a workout session or race, but a minimum of 45 minutes before. For best results, the prerace meal should be consumed 90 to 120 minutes before competition. Most of the top professionals (such as Jonathan Boyer and Thurlow Rogers) aim for a three-hour span between meal and race.

For several years it was thought that in order for proper hydration of the athlete to occur, the stomach must be able to empty quickly. It was also thought that glucose-enriched drinks interfered with the emptying process; therefore water was the only drink the cyclist should consume. Costill's research found this to be wrong. In fact, during long-term exercise, Costill found that it was quite effective for the athlete to consume high levels of glucose in a drink, and observed that it did not interfere with the emptying of the stomach as much as it improved efficiency by providing energy.

Every athlete is different, and has his or her own unique physiology and athletic goal. This is by no means the final and definitive word on nutrition. My strongest recommendation is for you to undertake a thorough study of nutrition in order to meet your specific and personal needs.

The pioneers of human-powered vehicle racing: Ron Skarin, Olympic racer, and Dr. Chester Kyle, aerodynamic engineer. The Skarin–Kyle combination set five world speed records at the Los Alamitos Naval Air Station in 1974. (Photo courtesy of Ron Skarin)

PART II
THE
TECHNOLOGICAL
EDGE

"To me, Francesco Moser's hour record will always be an asterisk record. He didn't break it because of superior athletics, he broke it because of superior technology."

—John Marino
Director, Race Across AMerica

When Francesco Moser broke Eddy Merckx's hour record in Mexico City, the worldwide governing body of the sport of cycling, the Union Cycliste Internationale (UCI), met in committee and wrung their hands in despair. Should they allow the record or shouldn't they? The issue was a critical one. The 1984 Los Angeles Olympic Games were only six months away and decisions made now could affect the outcome of the cycling competition, as well as the future of the sport.

The professed goal of bicycle racing, according to the UCI, is to test the athlete, not the equipment. The governing body wants to see equitability among cyclists. If a rider wins because of equipment that others do not have access to, then the goal of the race has not been met. On the other hand, one hates to bring back a technological dark age. After all, if this conservative philosophy had been adopted in the early decades of this century, we would still be riding single-speed, fixed gear, upright, steel-framed bikes, rolling on solid rubber tires. Progress is a compromise—you allow some changes, but not all. The multispeed derailleur was acceptable, the wraparound fairing was not.

Moser's record was accepted, and to maintain consistency the cycling teams in the Los Angeles Olympics were allowed to use their newly developed high-tech equipment. Of course, not all countries could afford the expense of outfitting their cycling teams with $60,000 bikes. Those that couldn't were at a disadvantage and protested loudly. Those that could took every available advantage and collected their medals. As Arthur Campbell, a member of the UCI Technical Commission noted: "It was a very disturbing time for us. We didn't know how to vote on this issue. In the end we just wished the whole affair would go away." Everyone would agree that equitability is the ultimate answer. But nearly everyone would also agree that technology simply can't progress at the rate of the poorest country. The prosperous will have greater success in competition, and others will not fare as well. In other words, the rich get richer and the poor . . .

As a compromise, the UCI has now adopted a stance that takes the marketplace into consideration. As a rule of thumb, a new product must be in the marketplace for one year, thus giving everyone equal access to it, before the UCI will allow it into competition. The year gives manufacturers an opportunity to compete and drive the prices down, allowing a reasonable number of competitors, teams, and countries access to equivalent technology. Competition then boils down to an event between athletes, not laboratory scientists.

In the history of cycling technology there are short periods of sudden growth and change in the sport, followed by long periods of stasis. Certain inventions mark the episodes of change—the pneumatic tire, the freewheel hub, and the derailleur, for instance. We are currently experiencing a monumental "speciation" period in the evolution of the bicycle. A new species is evolving, and the sport's conservative old guard, with an investment in the status quo, is resisting the change. But as Dr. Paul MacCready, winner of the Kremer Prize in human-powered flight for the Gossamer Condor and Gossamer Albatross, notes: "While the old way has value, innovation is inevitable. If your goal is raw speed on a bicycle, then innovation is necessary."

In this section, we will cover four general areas—Basics, Clothing, Safety, and Aerodynamics. Keeping in mind the twofold purpose, improvement for competitive performance and improvement for personal satisfaction, each of these topics will bring the reader up to date on the latest developments in the industry and sport of cycling.

73

Lon Haldeman and Susan Notorangelo, perhaps the most famous tandem couple in cycling, en route to setting the tandem transcontinental record. Both feel that tandem riding has greatly improved their individual cycling abilities. (Photo by Ken Haldeman.)

5
BASICS

"It's as easy as riding a bicycle—once you've learned it, you never forget." Ever heard that expression? Well, it's partially true. The basics of riding a bicycle are just that—basic. But if that's all there was to it you certainly wouldn't need a book on it. The basics we all learned as children about riding a bicycle have not changed. Everything else, however, has changed, and become considerably more complicated. The techniques of cycling are now a science.

Cycling is one of the most gadget-oriented sports in the world. While it could be said that for cycling all you need is a bike and a highway, that is saying a lot. There are many different types and brands of bikes, wheels, tires, cleated shoes, helmets, gloves, jerseys, shorts, socks, goggles, computers, components, rollers, trainers, caps, saddle pads—and the list goes on.

This chapter will deal with the bicycle itself, gearing, and basic training aids such as rollers and trainers.

THE BICYCLE

Though an entire book could be devoted to frame designs

and racing geometry theories, suffice it to say that in terms of a bicycle and its components, the better the equipment, the better the performance. In cycling equipment, as in most merchandise, you get what you pay for. Of course, there are the so-called "you're paying for the name" brands in both bicycles and components. In the past everyone seemed to agree that Campagnolo ("Campy") components were the *creme de la creme* of bicycle equipment. Everyone also agreed they were overpriced. But since they were the only game in town, the reputation sold the product. So revered were these components, in fact, that in Tullio Campagnolo's home country of Italy, where the manufacturing plant is located, as well as in France, home of the famed Tour de France, it has become a colloquial expression to describe a shapely woman as "Elle est tout Campagnolo," meaning she is well equipped in every way that counts.

But today things are different. With the recent explosion in the sport's growth, other quality-component manufacturers have been cashing in on the "quality first" credo espoused by Tullio a long time ago. The leader of this new wave of manufacturers, many of whom hail from the other side of the *other* ocean, is Shimano components, a Japanese manufacturer. Shimano's reputation is built not only on quality components but also innovative designs. Shimano was the first to design and manufacture aerodynamic components. In fact, they eventually may be held responsible for the boom in aerodynamic equipment and accessories that includes helmets, clothing, shoes, wheels, and the like. Their latest invention, sure to revolutionize the drive train of the bike, is the Shimano Index System, or S.I.S. The S.I.S. "clicks" the chain into each gear, or cog, so that you never have to adjust a gear, and you never miss a shift. So efficient is the S.I.S. shifting mechanism that I calculated I saved more than 2,000 shifts in the Race Across AMerica.

As for the bicycles themselves, they must bear stock components of the quality of Shimano, Campagnolo, Mavic, Sun Tour, Galli, or Maillard. So it comes down to the frame—the tubing, the brazing, the painting, and the final touches that make it a personal, handcrafted machine as opposed to an assembly-line production.

Paying $1,500–$2,000 does not guarantee a hand-built frame, crafted by the original designer himself. A highly rated, respectable name in racing bicycles is Bianchi, named after Eduardo Bianchi, who originally hand-brazed and painted every frame that left his shop. He died long ago, and Bianchi bicycles are now produced not only in Italy but in the Orient as well, where mass production can be done with cheaper labor costs. The top-of-the-line Bianchis are still high-quality bicycles, used by many professionals around the world, but sophisticated brazing machines and modern paint booths have replaced the one-man operations of the past.

When I first opened my shop, Shermer Cycles, in Arcadia, California, we carried a domestic brand, Schwinn, and a foreign brand, Peugeot. Today Schwinn manufactures most of their bicycles outside the United States. The "American-built" bike is now made in the Orient. And as to that finely built French machine, the Peugeot, it is still being put together in France, but it may soon be produced in the Orient as well.

A word to the wise: test-ride as many bicycles as possible before making your selection. Asking local experienced riders, or even professionals, what they prefer may bring you a tainted view. Professionals are under contract to ride for bicycle companies and will naturally recommend the model they are advertising during that racing season. To be fair, though, a top professional isn't going to ride any equipment that isn't top-of-the-line, because he primarily makes his reputation and money from his performance.

I was fortunate to have had two bike sponsors over the last six years who gave me a choice of different frames. My first major sponsorship came from Motobecane Bicycles, imported from France, which gave me a choice between the traditional steel frame and the innovative aluminum design by Vitus Tubing. Fortunately, I ignored the advice of

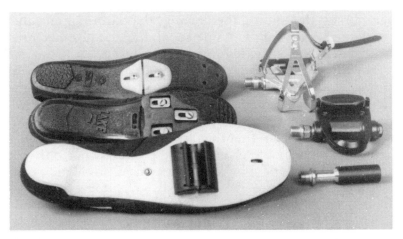

Three popular pedal systems currently in use. Top: Shimano's standard pedal-cage/toe-strap system—the most aerodynamic and comfortable of that type. Middle: the Look "safety" step-in pedal system—extremely efficient, lighter in weight than most standard pedal systems, and never allows the shoe to come out of the pedal. Bottom: the Aerolight pedal—a simple peg that is by far the lightest of all pedals, plus has the advantage of the Look pedal in safety and efficiency.

pessimists who warned that the aluminum frame would collapse, shatter, or be so flexible that you couldn't climb even an easy hill on it. Instead I went with my subjective feeling after riding the aluminum Prolight, as it was not only several pounds lighter but also was infinitely more comfortable on ultramarathon rides.

My current sponsor, Cycles Peugeot, made me almost the same offer. The company allowed me to choose between a steel frame and the carbon fiber design. Once again my subjective feeling was that the carbon fiber frame had all the advantages of the aluminum frame—it was light and comfortable. In addition, however, it seemed a bit stiffer, and therefore more efficient, without sacrificing the comfort. After logging more than 50,000 miles on the carbon fiber Peugeot, I can conclude that it is even more comfortable than the Prolight. This correlates with the research findings on tennis rackets and golf clubs made of the same material. Apparently the carbon material has a damping effect on vibration, whether it is picked up from a tennis ball by the racket, a miss-hit by the golf club, or from highways that were designed for fat-tire cars traveling at 60 miles per hour, not skinny-tire bicycles moving 20 miles per hour. Especially in long-distance riding, road vibration can take its toll on the body after hours and sometimes days of constant abuse.

A road-test article in *Bicycling* magazine last year rated the Peugeot carbon fiber bicycle quite high. Not only did it pass all of the standard frame stiffness tests, it was extremely comfortable to ride, over any distance.

Jonathan Boyer, the winner of the 1985 Race Across AMerica, and the first American rider to break into the elite European racing circles, including the Tour de France, rides an aluminum frame. Boyer claims it is just as stiff as a steel frame and more comfortable.

Everyone is different, however, and you must test the different materials yourself. Correct bike size is important. A 27-inch frame is not the size you want unless you are six and a half feet tall. Many people mistake the wheel size for the frame size. Most 10- and 12-speed bicycles have 27-inch wheels. The greatest variation in bike size is in the frame, which may be as small as 17 inches and as large as 25 inches, as measured from the middle of the bottom bracket to the middle of the top tube where it joins the seat tube. There are many sophisticated and impressive formulas for calculating the exact bike size you should use. These usually involve inseam length in relation to torso length and many other measurements. A fast and simple test is to straddle the top tube of a bike with both feet flat on the ground. The top tube should be between an inch and two inches from the groin area. If contact is made, the frame is too big. If it is three inches or more below the groin, the frame is too small. (See sections later in this chapter for further information on correct positioning and comfort on a bike.)

GEARING

One of the most difficult areas of cycling to master is the gearing system, especially for those who are not mechanically minded. Bikes have different gearing systems, different size gears, different locations for shifters, and so on. Some rear clusters have 5 speeds, most have 6, but some have 7. There are 1-speeds, 3-speeds, 5-speeds, 10-speeds, 12-speeds, 15-speeds, 18-speeds, and 21-speeds. Do you need 21 gears? Isn't 12 speeds enough? What does it all mean?

Most people learn about gearing systems through experience alone. All cyclists know that the shifter on the left side of the bike controls the front derailleur and the shifter on the right side controls the rear derailleur. A normal 12-speed bicycle has two chainrings connected to the pedals' crank arms, and a six-speed cluster, or freewheel, on the rear wheel. The front derailleur shifts the chain from the small chainring to the big chainring and back. The rear derailleur shifts the chain up and down the six cogs, from the lowest to the highest gear and back. Thus, you have six choices of gears in the rear and two choices in the front—a total of 12 gear alternatives.

The object of the drivetrain is to propel the bicycle forward under the power of the legs. On flat ground, this is relatively easy at low speeds, but as rolling hills and mountainous grades loom ahead on the highway, you must shift gears according to your strength level to negotiate the climb. The object of a gearing system is to allow you to maintain a fairly steady pedaling cadence. This can easily be calculated by counting the number of times one leg goes around in a complete circle in 10 seconds, then multiplying by six. Sixty revolutions per minute (rpm) is a slow to medium cadence; 80 rpm is a medium cadence; 100 rpm or more is a high cadence. It is generally agreed that for good aerobic exercise one should maintain a medium to high cadence, approximately 80–120 rpm. This keeps the heart rate high and makes for a quality workout.

The gearing system becomes important in maintaining

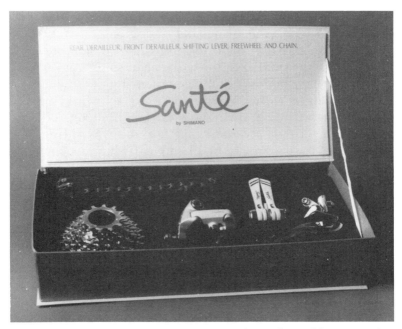

The newest gearing systems are aerodynamic and incorporate the S.I.S. index, or click, shifting mechanism that allow perfect shifts every time. It won't be long before friction-style shifting mechanisms will be a thing of the past.

that steady cadence on a rolling or hilly course. If you begin to climb a hill and your cadence slows, shifting to a lower gear will restore your original cadence. When you begin to descend and your speed increases dramatically, you will need to shift to a higher gear in order to keep pedaling.

Gears are classified by the number of teeth. A "42" chainring has 42 teeth on it. A "14" cog is a gear in the freewheel that has 14 teeth on it. Cyclists typically refer to their gears in these terms. One might say, "I was climbing in my 42 by 19, but it was so steep I had to shift to my 21." This means the cyclist was riding in the 42-tooth chainring on the front and 19-tooth cog in the back. Since the hill was steep, she had to shift to a lower gear, in this case the 21-tooth cog, in order to keep a reasonable cadence.

The more teeth there are in the front chainrings, the bigger or higher the gear, and the more resistance in pedaling. In the rear, the opposite is true. The more teeth the cog has, the smaller or lower the gear, so the easiest gear to pedal in would be the smallest chainring and the largest cog. The most difficult gear to pedal in would be the opposite—the big chainring and the smallest cog. When a cyclist is relating how hard and fast she was riding, she might say, "I was in my 52 by 13 and really hammering!"

Gearing systems are not sequential in design, although many novices mistakenly believe this to be so. This would mean that, on a 12-speed bike, gears 1-6 refer to the position of the chain on the small chainring, with the shifting occurring on the freewheel in the order 1-2-3-4-5-6. Gears 6-12 would then be the position of the chain on the big chainring, and the gears simply shift down the freewheel 7-8-9-10-11-12. This couldn't be further from the truth.

With the 12-speed arrangement below, shifting up through the gears from smallest to biggest actually requires seven changes of the front derailleur and 12 changes of the rear derailleur. Obviously, this isn't simple Let's say your current gearing system is set up as follows: chainrings—54 and 42; freewheel—13, 14, 15, 17, 19, 21. The actual ranking from 1 to 12, or smallest to biggest gear:

1.	42×21	7.	42×14
2.	42×19	8.	54×17
3.	42×17	9.	42×13
4.	54×21	10.	54×15
5.	42×15	11.	54×14
6.	54×19	12.	54×13

What if your gearing system is different? How can you rank your own system to decide on an appropriate gear? A gear-ratio chart can help you. The gear-ratio chart below plots the number of teeth on the rear sprocket on the horizontal axis and the number of teeth on the chainrings on the vertical axis. To find the number of gear-inches, which will be the method of ranking the gears, correlate the chainring size with the cog size and read across the graph. For instance, a 42 chainring with a 21 cog is a 54-inch gear. From the explanation above, you would expect the 42×19 gear to be larger in inches. A quick check of the table shows it to be 59.7 inches—a larger gear.

Gear-inches is a term that originated in the late 1800s when the "high-wheeler," or "ordinary" bicycle, was commonly used. Since the pedals were attached to the large front wheel and there was no chain or freewheel, the gear-inches represented the diameter of that large wheel. An ordinary bike with a 54-inch gear had a front wheel that was 54 inches in diameter. In other words, the larger the wheel, the farther the bicyle would travel with each pedal stroke. The larger the wheel, the harder it would be to pedal up a hill. Thus a small gear, or small wheel, was needed for a hilly ride.

Translated into today's chains and freewheels, the distance you travel with each pedal stroke will depend on the circumference of the wheel and on the gear-inches. To calculate the circumference of the wheel, multiply its diameter by pi (3.1416). A 27-inch wheel has a circumference of 84.82 inches. Thus, on a 27-inch ordinary bicycle, one pedal stroke would net you a distance of 84.82 inches, or a little over seven feet. To calculate how far you travel with each pedal stroke on a modern bicycle, multiply the number of gear-inches (from the gear-ratio chart) by pi. If you are in the 42×21 gear, you would multiply 54 by 3.1416, and the result is 169.65 inches, or 14.14 feet traveled.

The gear chart should be used to adjust your bicycle's gears. If you are going on a training ride, a race, or a tour that is extremely hilly, then you will need a gearing system that has low enough gear-inches to accommodate those climbs. Most of the adjusting can be done on the freewheel. Rarely do the chainrings get switched, because it is not as simple a task as replacing the rear wheel with a different cluster.

A standard circular chainring is contrasted with an "elliptical" chainring. It is scientifically designed to maximize the number of teeth in action during the power stroke and minimize the number of teeth in action during the recovery stroke.

For the most part, the fitter you are, the less variation you need between gears. Most competitive cyclists can get by with a 52 × 42 chainring set up with a 13–21 freewheel structure. The 54-inch lowest gear can get a fit cyclist over almost any hill. In fact, Jonathan Boyer has boasted that he "straight-blocked" America in the RAAM in 1985, meaning he used a 13–18 freewheel, or only one tooth difference between each gear.

Some cyclists like to have a slightly larger chainring. Some move up to a 53 or even a 54, particularly if they like to push big gears at a lower rpm. Others prefer to spin high rpm, so they may move down to a 50.

Occasionally one finds a chainring smaller than a 42. Tourists who carry heavy packs and mountain bike racers frequently need a chainring as small as a 36 to reach a mountaintop. Some touring bikes even sport three chainrings to give extra gear options. Many, if not most, tandems have a triple chainring set up for those extra big hills, which tandems are notoriously slow at climbing. I have an interesting setup on my tandem, using the S.I.S. shifters with a 38, 48, 53 Biopace, and a seven-speed 13, 14, 15, 17, 19, 21, 23 cluster on the rear. It's a perfect combination for tandem riding, especially if the stoker and driver are both strong riders.

Occasionally, a 21-speed setup produces duplication of gears. For instance, a 52 × 28 is a 50.1-inch gear. A 42 × 22 is a 51.5-inch gear. The difference is so small you could never distinguish between the two gears.

Experience and the use of the gear-ratio chart will help you decide which system is best suited to your conditioning and cycling needs.

BASIC TRAINING AIDS

BIKE COMPUTERS

A reliable bike computer is a must for accurate feedback on exactly how you're progressing. As you become better conditioned, the differences on a day-to-day basis will become smaller, with your average miles per hour only changing by tenths. I recommend that the computer you acquire, therefore, be able to calculate average miles per

GEAR RATIO CHART

Number of Teeth on Freewheel

Number of Teeth on Chainrings

	12	13	14	15	16	17	18	19	20	21	22	23	24	25	26	27	28
40	90.0	83.1	77.1	72.0	67.5	63.5	60.0	56.8	54.0	51.4	49.1	47.0	45.0	43.2	41.5	40.0	38.6
41	92.2	85.2	79.1	73.8	69.2	65.1	61.5	58.3	55.3	52.7	50.3	48.1	46.1	44.3	42.7	41.3	40.1
42	94.5	87.2	81.0	75.6	70.9	66.7	63.0	59.7	56.7	54.0	51.5	49.3	47.3	45.4	43.6	42.0	40.5
43	96.7	89.3	82.9	77.4	72.6	68.3	64.5	61.1	58.0	55.3	52.8	50.5	48.4	46.4	44.6	43.0	41.4
44	100.0	91.4	84.9	79.2	74.3	69.9	66.0	62.5	59.4	56.6	54.0	51.7	49.5	47.5	45.7	44.0	42.4
45	101.2	93.5	86.8	81.0	75.9	71.5	67.5	63.9	60.8	57.9	55.2	52.8	50.6	48.6	46.7	45.0	43.4
46	103.5	95.5	88.7	82.8	77.6	73.1	69.0	65.4	62.1	59.1	56.5	54.0	51.8	49.7	47.8	46.0	44.4
47	105.7	97.6	90.6	84.6	79.3	74.6	70.5	66.8	63.4	60.4	57.7	55.2	52.9	50.8	48.8	47.0	45.3
48	108.0	99.7	92.6	86.4	81.0	76.2	72.0	68.2	64.8	61.7	58.9	56.3	54.0	51.8	49.9	48.0	46.3
49	110.2	101.8	94.5	88.2	82.7	77.8	73.5	69.6	66.1	63.0	60.1	57.5	55.1	52.9	50.9	49.0	47.2
50	112.5	103.8	96.4	90.0	84.4	79.4	75.0	71.1	67.5	64.3	61.4	58.7	56.3	54.0	51.9	50.0	48.2
51	114.7	105.9	98.4	91.8	86.1	81.0	76.5	72.5	68.8	65.6	62.6	59.9	57.4	55.1	53.0	51.0	49.1
52	117.0	108.0	100.3	93.6	87.8	82.6	78.0	73.9	70.2	66.9	63.8	61.0	58.5	56.2	54.0	52.0	50.1
53	119.3	110.1	102.2	95.4	89.4	84.2	79.5	75.3	71.5	68.1	65.0	62.2	59.6	57.2	55.0	53.0	51.1
54	121.5	112.2	104.1	97.2	91.1	85.8	81.0	76.7	72.9	69.4	66.3	63.4	60.8	58.3	56.1	54.0	52.0
55	123.7	114.2	106.2	99.0	92.8	87.3	82.5	78.1	74.5	70.7	67.5	64.5	61.8	59.4	57.1	55.0	53.0
56	126.0	116.3	108.0	100.9	94.5	88.9	84.0	79.5	75.6	72.0	68.7	65.7	63.0	60.4	58.1	56.0	54.0

hour to one or two decimal places. Other functions that are important are current miles per hour, miles traveled on the current ride, and elapsed time. Other functions that some computers can perform that are not as critical are such things as cadence, gear-inches, and cumulative miles traveled (over days, weeks, months, or even years if your computer lasts that long). One of the biggest problems with most of the bike computers is reliability. It is not at all unusual for a computer to go blank when it is hot, cold, or on a bumpy road. Rarely have I ridden 300 miles without some malfunction rendering the computer useless.

TRAINING LOG

The training log or training chart at the end of Chapter 1 will suffice for logging miles ridden in the course of weeks, months, and a year. To record other information, any notebook will do. Get into the habit of logging your food intake, weight, miles ridden, time elapsed, average miles per hour, and anything else you think is pertinent. It even might be useful to set up a subjective rating scale of how you feel on a day-to-day basis. A 1-to-10 scale might work, with the 10 being reserved for those exceptional days when you drop the local champion on a ride, and the 1 being reserved for the days when you turn around and go back home after 15 minutes!

ROLLERS

Rollers are indoor training devices built so that a bicycle can be balanced on them while you pedal. They are constructed with one roller under the front wheel and two rollers under the rear wheel. To ride rollers requires a balancing act that takes a bit of practice. One twitch of the front wheel will send you flying to the floor. Once mastered, however, rollers can be an easy and effective training method during inclement weather, or nighttime riding sessions.

Most rollers are built so that even in the highest gear rpm will remain relatively high with little effort. I use the Kreitler roller system, and when riding in my 53 × 12 gear, I easily hold my cadence at 100-plus rpm. This is great

Though riding on rollers has been rejected as a viable training tool because of their low resistance (unless a turbo device is attached for creating wind drag), it is an excellent method for teaching smooth pedaling style and balance. When riding rollers you must pedal in circles, not squares.

training for spinning, balance, and holding the bicycle in a straight line.

To simulate riding on the highway, though, requires an adaptation to the rollers called a wind system. On the Kreitler roller system you can add a turbo wind device that is driven by the rollers. The circular blades cut through the air, causing friction, thus drag on the rollers. This produces a much more difficult workout because you must pedal harder to maintain the same rpm. In addition, the fan is directed toward the cyclist, creating a wind that is the equivalent of riding on the highway at 20 miles per hour. You can buy an inexpensive blower and rig it to the roller system if you can't afford the conventional unit.

With the wind system, riding in high gear at a cadence of 100-plus requires a tremendous output of energy, thus a high-quality workout. With the Kreitler wind system, there is even an adjustable "door" to vary the amount of air that is sucked into the turbo blades, thus allowing you to vary the amount of drag, or the intensity of the workout.

WIND TRAINERS

Wind trainers are different from rollers in that most of them are designed to have the front wheel removed and locked into place in the trainer. The wheel is held in place by a vertical post that has a quick release skewer. The rear wheel of the bike rests on a roller, and connected to that are two turbo wind drums with blades that produce friction as they cut through the air. The friction creates drag on the roller, making for a more difficult training session.

On wind trainers, the faster your cadence the more difficult it becomes to pedal. To maintain high rpm, a high output of energy is required.

The advantage of the wind trainer over rollers is that you have to work harder for the same rpm. The disadvantage is that the front wheel is locked in place so that no balance is required, which means you miss the training that rollers give you for riding in a straight line. The wind trainer does, however, allow you to stand up out of the saddle and practice climbing hills in this fashion. To stand up on the pedals on rollers is next to impossible at any reasonable speed.

STATIONARY BIKES

Stationary bikes are constructed with a large wheel or drum that rotates under the power of the spinning pedals.

Friction is applied to the wheel with rubber brakes or a nylon band around the circumference of the wheel. There is usually a knob that allows you to control the amount of friction, thus varying the intensity of the workout.

Stationary bikes have the advantage of not requiring any time or effort to set them up. With rollers and wind trainers you have to use your own bike, and in the case of the wind trainer, you must remove the front wheel, which prevents the use of a bike computer, since most of them operate by means of a rotating magnet attached to the front wheel. (Many bike computer companies provide an interchangeable unit for picking up the magnetic pulses from the rear wheel.) Virtually all stationary bikes have a speedometer and an odometer to measure miles per hour and miles traveled.

Another advantage is that stationary bikes tend to be a bit more stable and allow you to ride out of the saddle without much sway. I have witnessed Lon Haldeman ride a Monarch stationary bike for hours at a time, alternately sitting and standing up out of the saddle. While standing, he sometimes rides with no hands on the bars to stabilize himself, using just one hand holding on to a beam in the ceiling. It appears that this method builds up even stronger leg muscles as it isolates those muscle groups to concentrate on only one movement. You can also rig up a wind blower to a stationary bike, as Lon and his wife, Susan, have done in their basement, to make riding the bike tolerable for any reasonable duration.

With this system one is handicapped by the inability to move. When you are on the road the wind cools you off, and the time passes quickly as you accelerate down hills, fly through hairpin corners, and enjoy the local geography. Riding indoors is, to say the least, limiting in scope. But one need not subject oneself to the rigors of a Mike Secrest training session in a five-foot by eight-foot darkened closet.

Riding indoors can actually be enjoyable and productive. For instance, I use the time not only to get a quality workout but to listen to lecture tapes, watch videotapes of television documentaries, or even let the mind vegetate on a diet of "Star Trek" and "Twilight Zone" reruns. If you set it up right, you can even have your telephone next to the bike and make calls while you ride. This becomes more difficult, of course, when you are riding strenuously.

HOW TO GO FASTER

Speeds in bike competition never approach those of human-powered vehicle races, with the exception of steeply graded downhills. The reason continues to be restrictions set down by the UCI. Improvements must come within the UCI's parameters, which have recently been expanded to include items such as disk wheels and aero helmets.

Other means of increasing speed and performance are:

Recumbent Bicycles—The rider is in a supine position, which provides a 15 to 20 percent decrease in air resistance.

ZZipper Fairing—A small, light, and easy-to-attach fairing that fits on the front handlebars can increase speed as much as 2.5 miles per hour.

Tandem—A bicycle built for two allows the stoker, or back rider, to "draft" off the front rider, so that 20 percent less power per rider is required to maintain the same speed as a single-rider bike. These effects are especially noticeable on flat ground and downhills. On a long climb, however, the added weight more than cancels the double power output, resulting in tandems typically getting dropped off the back of a pack of single-rider bikes. There are a few exceptions. If both riders have a high power-to-weight ratio (that is, they are both lightweight and extremely strong), and are experienced riding together, they can climb as well as single riders. Pete Penseyres and Rob Templin are such a pair. In the 1985 Arizona Challenge, which featured more than 20,000 feet of climbing in 325 miles, Penseyres and Templin beat Jim Elliot, John Royer, and me.

Tandem riding builds more upper-body strength because the bike is heavier and more difficult to handle on hills, corners, and at stoplights. Tandem riding also builds a consistent cadence, because holding a steady pace is essential in keeping the double-weighted machine moving up and down hills. You tend to stay seated more on a tandem than on a single bike, so it toughens your rear and helps prevent saddle sores when riding a single bike.

On the subjective side, it is also fun because you get stares from passersby, who might exclaim, "Hey, there goes one of those bicycles built for two!" Tandems are fun in a pack of riders because it is easy to stay toward the front. You tend to pull the pack along for long periods of time, and on downhills you can drop riders effortlessly. The best part about tandem riding, however, is not the speed but the interaction with your partner. Whether your pedals are "in sync" or "out of sync" (that is, whether they are parallel or 90 degrees out of phase), there is a harmony in the synchronized movement of two people pedaling in tandem.

Angel Rodrigues, builder of Rodrigues Tandems in Seattle, claims that tandem riding with a member of the opposite sex, can be better than, well . . . sex! It's a great way to spend an afternoon with your spouse or dating partner, and if one person rides more than the other, and their skills are not equal, the tandem becomes the great equalizer. Andy Gilmour, builder of Gilmour Tandems (and single-bike frames) in Tucson, and Sue Casey, a top USCF (United States Cycling Federation) road racer, recently teamed up, and with only one day of riding experience, won the tandem category in the 1986 El Tour de Tucson. Their single-bike cycling skills quickly transferred to the tandem for a successful and enjoyable 110 miles.

As a training aid for the serious cyclist, tandem riding adds miles to your base for the year by getting you out on the bike at times when you don't want to but your partner does. Lon Haldeman claims that ever since he got his tandem he rides at least 5,000 more miles a year than when he was riding single bikes only. For me, when I take the tandem out for one of the regular local training rides, I look forward to it as something that is fun instead of work. It is almost like a vacation away from the single bike, and yet I still get in my training miles.

Tires—Bald versus treaded has been hotly debated re-

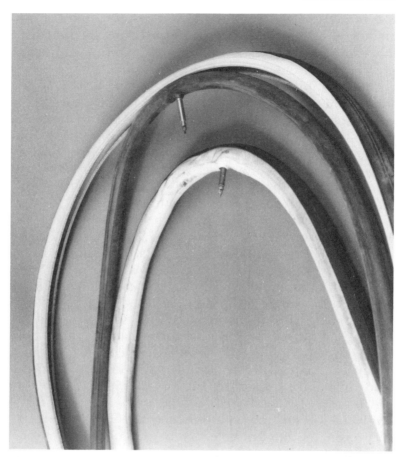

A sew-up tire, top, is contrasted with a standard clincher. Sew-ups house the inner tube inside the tire itself, whereas the clincher is a two-piece design. According to Dr. Chester Kyle, "Sew-up wheels are nearly a pound lighter per wheel than wired-ons [clinchers]. Light weight is very critical to a racer." (Photo by Michael Coles)

cently, with the evidence still inconclusive regarding rolling resistance. The manufacturers of the new bald tires have provided compelling evidence for the efficacy of this innovation. Dr. Chester Kyle, however, notes that tread or no tread, sew-up tires are still superior to clinchers because air pressure in sew-ups can greatly exceed those limits set by

92

the manufacturers of clinchers. It is important to note, however, that for most riders clincher tires can hold more air pressure than they will ever put in them. In addition, Dr. Kyle notes that "sew-up wheels are nearly a pound lighter per wheel than wired-ons. This is probably the main reason that clinchers can't compete, even more important than the higher possible pressure. Light weight is critical to a racer."

White clothing reflects heat and keeps the body cool in even the hottest weather.

"If you look good and dress well, you don't need a purpose in life."

—Robert Pante
fashion consultant

6
CLOTHING

There are many considerations when selecting proper clothing for a bicycle ride or race, not the least of which is looks. Whether they are willing to admit it or not, cyclists are vain athletes. They like to look good. Part of the aura that surrounds a cycling event is the color and glitter of the riders and their machines. A bicycle race is one of the most popular "poster sports" because it is so colorful. And let's fess up—while shaving one's legs is justified by aerodynamics, crashes, and massages, the biggest single reason is because it looks good and everyone does it. I don't know if it is the same with other sports, but in cycling if you do not fit the part and play the role with the appropriate gear and uniforms, you will never be accepted into the elite inner circle.

But to be fair, it isn't that everyone is conforming merely to be accepted into the group. Bicycle clothing—jerseys, shorts, socks, jackets, tights, and the like—does look good. It's fun to wear, especially for men, who otherwise, in macho-American style, are not supposed to take an interest in fashion and other such "feminine" concerns.

Three popular models of eye protection: the Oakley Factory Pilots, the Oakley Blades, and the Gargoyles (a.k.a. "Terminator" glasses). (Photo by Michael Coles)

Television has brought into the American living room what the top pros wear in competition. The Tour de France, the Coors Classic, the Giro D'Italia, and the Race Across AMerica, all televised nationally, have given the weekend rider the role models to emulate. After the Tour de France was broadcast on CBS last summer, a rash of La Vie Claire jerseys was seen on every club ride for months. (Greg LeMond, the winner of the 1986 Tour, rides for the brightly colored La Vie Claire professional team.) After the 1985 Race Across AMerica, advertisements ran in national cycling publications urging readers to buy Jonathan Boyer's "RAAM" jersey.

It is not unusual to see cyclists all over America sporting jerseys and shorts plastered with Italian, French, and Belgian company names that most can't even pronounce, let alone translate. But it doesn't matter, because when you look good you feel good. And when you feel good, you ride better. But even if you don't *really* ride faster, you will at least feel like you are. Clothing, however, *can* affect cycling speed and performance.

Leaving fashion aside, the *type* of clothing can have as much of an effect on speed, efficiency, and comfort as any other variable in the sport. Dr. Chester Kyle reports that in wind tunnel tests, "sloppy or loose-fitting clothing can raise the total wind drag by 10 percent or more; hence, more can probably be gained in choosing the proper clothing

96

than by any other legal means in racing." Kyle applies this principle to the 4,000-meter pursuit on a velodrome, where loose clothing can slow a rider's time by as much as two seconds. Since most 4,000-meter pursuit events are won or lost by less than two seconds, the choice of clothing is critical.

For starters, a skintight Lycra-Spandex jersey, or a jersey/ shorts one-piece combination, is far superior to the traditional wool or cotton jersey and shorts. If it is possible to get by without pockets, all the better. In short criteriums and velodrome races this is no problem. In longer criteriums, most road races (at least for men), and all ultramarathon cycling events, carrying food is necessary. For competition, if you can get your hands on a "rubberized" skinsuit, like those used by the U.S. Cycling Team in the 1984 Olympics, even more time can be shaved off the overall performance. Though Dr. Kyle has noted that "for events over five minutes, Lycra is nearly as low in drag and gives adequate ventilation and cooling."

Further, skinsuits are extremely comfortable. Because they are form-fitting they don't shift around on your body. Lycra shorts don't "creep" up and cause chafing the way wool and cotton shorts are known to do. I don't even own a pair of wool or cotton shorts anymore. And, weather permitting, I usually (though not always) prefer Lycra jerseys over most others. Lycra quickly wicks off perspiration, keeping you dry most of the time. Lycra "spider suits," which are skinsuits with full length arms and legs, are extremely aerodynamic because they cover leg and arm hair, in case they haven't already been shaved. Research does support the notion that head and body hair has a noticeable effect on wind drag. In serious racing, time trials, and record attempts, arm and leg hair should be shaved, and head and facial hair clipped. An aerodynamic helmet is better than a bald head, and will protect the brain as well. The spider suit covers body hair, but if the temperature is too high or too low, that approach won't work. Finally, skinsuits exhibit sponsors' names clearly and sharply—an important consideration if you want to make money at this game.

There are instances, however, when Lycra skinsuits and jerseys are not appropriate. For most of cycling's history the traditional cycling togs were usually made of wool. Wool provides warmth, maintains body heat even when wet, breathes, and can absorb up to 16 percent of its own weight in moisture without losing its insulating ability. Wool is "fuzzy," and the tiny air pockets within the material hold heat. Up until this decade almost everyone either wore wool or cotton. And if it was cold or wet outside, you definitely wore wool.

Wool does have its disadvantages. Colors run. Jerseys and shorts shrink when put in a dryer. If hung outside they take enormous periods of time to dry, unless it's hot, in which case you probably don't want to wear the jersey anyway. The biggest problem with wool is that it just doesn't fit quite like Lycra. Wool is not form-fitting, unless it has shrunk, which usually makes it uncomfortably tight.

Cotton was the next innovation in clothing, particularly for warm-weather cycling. Cotton has five times the thermal conductivity over many other fibers. In the Race Across AMerica, which takes place during the summer months when temperatures can easily exceed 110 degrees, I have always either worn cotton or Lycra. Cotton is superior to Lycra in thermal conductivity, but not as form-fitting and comfortable. Lon Haldeman frequently dons cotton jerseys in the RAAM and other ultramarathon events.

Cotton, however, is not so efficient for winter riding. Wet cotton transfers heat up to 200 times faster than dry cotton. I have had several bouts with hypothermia, all of which occurred in winter storms while wearing cotton jerseys. Technology now has entered the clothing scene. Where the ability of a garment to insulate was thought to be exclusively a function of its thickness, it is now known that the fiber's resistance to wind, reaction to moisture, and ability to conduct heat all play a role. There are now many synthetics on the market that are superior to both wool and cotton. Polypropylene, for example, is an excellent insulator because of its low specific gravity (0.91—the lower the figure, the better). It also breathes more efficiently and is lighter, even when wet, which it has a difficult time becoming. Polypropylene has a hydrophobic quality, literally translated as "fear of water." Water molecules do not mix well with the giant synthetic molecules which make up polypropylene and other synthetic fabrics. Finally, polypropylene dries quickly—excellent for areas where it rains on and off, and where the temperature can fluctuate many times during a long ride.

Pile, a combination of nylon and polyester, is similar to polypropylene in its ability to resist water. It is easy to wash and dry, and is an excellent insulator, making it an ideal winter fabric.

One of the finest wet-weather cycling garments is Gore-Tex, developed by W.L. Gore & Associates. A sponsor of the RAAM in 1983, the company supplied every cyclist with a Gore-Tex rain suit, including pants, jacket, and hood. Though it didn't rain during that race, subsequent years found the RAAM riders constantly soaked. In 1985 it rained every day but the first and the last. On the average it rained 12 to 14 hours a day. While the temperatures were not that debilitating, being constantly wet causes serious skin problems, especially where it meets the saddle. For the first and only time in my cycling career, I developed serious, open wounds on my rear that caused my overall speed to decrease significantly because I had to stop at least half-a-dozen times a day to rewrap the dressing. The Gore-Tex jacket, however, kept my upper body dry and warm.

Gore-Tex is the best fabric for wet-weather riding because polytetrafluorethylene, commonly known as PTFE, will resist water at up to 110 pounds of pressure before it gives in. No rainstorm will ever exceed that figure. But what makes Gore-Tex so special is that it is not only waterproof but also breathes. The pores of the membrane are larger than the individual molecules of perspiration, yet smaller than water droplets from rain, thus allowing some heat to escape (preventing overheating from a "saunalike" condition) while keeping water out. It is recommended that you don't wear too many clothes under the Gore-Tex garment, because the fabric itself will do the job.

Finally, the color of clothing can make a difference in temperature control. The rule of thumb is simple—light colors in the summer, dark colors in the winter. Research has shown that black material can absorb as much as 95 percent of the electromagnetic energy from the sun, while white material may only absorb 30 percent. Intermediate colors average around 50 percent. The "albedo," or ability to reflect the sun's rays, is the critical issue with clothing colors.

RAAM riders are especially conscious of this because of the extremes of temperatures. I have ridden in temperatures as high as 118 degrees and as low as 27 degrees—in the same race! Every year I have had my clothing sponsor, Kucharik Bicycle Clothing, make me an all-white Lycra-Spandex skinsuit. Though I have frequently experienced heat prostration in training rides and races preceding the RAAM, I have never succumbed to the sun in the race itself. This is partially due to Kucharik's white skinsuit. (Acclimation to environmental conditions will be covered in a later chapter.) I don't recommend an all-white skinsuit, however, because when they get wet (from either perspiration or dousing), the material becomes rather transparent!

The sport of triathlon has given cycling clothing a whole new range of color and fabrics. Triathletes, not chained to tradition (how could they be, the sport's only been around for slightly more than a decade), have come up with some of the most creative designs ever seen on a cyclist. But in addition to the fashion aspects, many triathlon cycling shorts and jerseys have incorporated mesh side panels, vis-à-vis running singlets. They are excellent for warm-weather cycling, look good, and are available at most quality bicycle shops.

CLOTHING

You need not be confined to *only* white jerseys in the summer and *only* black jerseys in the winter. While there are many good-looking white and black designs, there is a host of intermediate colors to choose from that are almost as effective in temperature control. Remember, the important part is the back of the jersey, since that is what is most exposed. Side panels and the front of the jersey can vary in color considerably without affecting overall body temperature.

John Howard shows that goggles are not only more aerodynamic but also eliminate eye strain caused by wind, debris, and sun.

"If you could see some of the brain injuries I've seen as a neurosurgeon, the helmet controversy wouldn't even be an issue."

—F. Clifford Roberson, M.D.

"If you've got a $10 head, then wear a $10 helmet."

—Bell Helmets advertisement

7
SAFETY

When Dean Fisher, vice president of Bell Helmets, addressed what promised (but failed) to be the most controversial issue of the two-day congress on the scientific aspects of cycling at the 1986 World Cycling Championships—the hard-shell helmet rule—most were surprised by the conciliatory nature of the audience. It almost seemed that the acceptability of wearing a hard-shell helmet may not be as slow in coming as expected. Six months before, however, the sport was up in arms. Riders threatened to boycott races. Promoters considered holding their events without a USCF sanction. And the USCF was almost unable to obtain insurance to cover such a "dangerous" sport.

At the congress, absolutely no one in the audience or panel (which also consisted of Carl Leusenkamp, a USCF national coach; Miroslav Slavic, M.D., a UCI representative; and neurosurgeon F. Clifford Roberson) suggested that riders should not wear an approved safety helmet. The statistics and test results on helmets are so convincing that to disagree would make one seem irrational. Even the old "pro choice" argument was rejected, in that our litigious

*The evolution of the bicycle helmet. From left to right: the
leather hairnet gave way to the first hard-shell helmet, the Bell
Biker, which was improved in looks and effectiveness with the
V1-Pro. The latest helmet designs also take aerodynamics into
consideration, as shown here in the Bell Stratos.*

society, bound in the chains of exorbitant insurance claims
and premiums, has made one man's free choice another
man's costly burden.

Many riders still choose to ride without a helmet in
training, but all must use helmets in amateur races, or they
cannot race. I must confess my own bias, even before the
ruling, has always been toward wearing a helmet, under all
conditions—racing or training. But I am not without
sympathy for the "real racer" who loves to cruise down the
highway with the sun on his face and the wind blowing
through his hair. It is an incredibly free feeling. You look
better and you feel better. When you ride to a restaurant or
to a friend's house your hair is dry and blown back, instead
of sweaty and matted down from helmet use. Some have
accused me of promoting helmets because of my sponsorship with Bell Helmets. Nothing could be further from the
truth. I wore a helmet before I was sponsored by Bell. And
I *always* wear my helmet today, even on solo training rides,
during the day, during the week, when I *know* I won't be
seen by anyone. My sympathies with the no-helmet crowd
are greatly outweighed by the safety aspects of wearing a
helmet. The freedom is simply not worth the price to be
paid with one fatal fall or accident.

The statistics are startling. More than 1,000 cycling deaths that occur each year in the United States are caused by collisions with automobiles, and in 80 percent of these, death is due to head trauma.

The energy of falling objects is measured in terms of g's, the same term used by astronauts to describe the force their rocket needs to escape the earth's gravitational field. When a falling object impacts against a surface its sudden deceleration is also given a g value. A cyclist traveling at 15 to 20 miles per hour who takes a typical fall directly over the handlebars into a fixed object will "decelerate," or impact his head, at an unbelievable 1,000 g's! Think about that statistic relative to the g force of only *three* that the space shuttle astronauts experience during launch. The cyclist would surely die under such an impact.

(I have a Bell V1-Pro hanging in my bike shop in the helmet section whose liner in the front is smashed down to about one-quarter of an inch. This was the result of an extremely forceful collision between Interstate 5 in California and my forehead. Interstate 5 was the victor, but there was no victim—the liner absorbed all the energy of the deceleration.)

A hard-shell helmet that contains an expanded polystyrene liner, or EPS (similar to the Styrofoam used in disposable cups), will absorb almost the entire energy of the impact, resulting in little or no head/brain injury. My wife worked as the public relations director of Bell Helmets for four years and brought home hundreds of letters from people whose doctors told them they would be dead now if it were not for their safety helmet. It may feel good not to wear a helmet, but it has to be the most reckless act a cyclist could *ever* perform. As John Howard likes to say, "There are only two types of cyclists—those who *have* fallen and those who are *going* to fall." One must be prepared for the inevitable.

The texture of the brain has been likened to jello. As Dr. Roberson observed at the top of this chapter, when you've seen a damaged brain there is no helmet controversy. In selecting a helmet, look for the ANSI or Snell approved stickers. ANSI, the American National Standards Institute, has established its Z90.4 standard, which calls for helmets to be dropped from a height of one meter, or 3.28 feet. Each helmet must be dropped four times, making contact on the front, back, and both sides. The helmet is dropped twice on a flat surface, called an anvil, and twice on a hemispheric anvil. The standards of the Snell Memorial Foundation (named for a fellow named Snell, who died of head injuries) are not quite as stringent as ANSI's. The impact must not exceed a minimum "g" load at which a loss of consciousness and memory is possible.

At the time of this writing, the helmets that have passed the standards include (alphabetically): AC Targa Sport, Avenir, Bailen, Bell Biker, Bell L'il Bell Shell, Bell Tourlite, Bell V1 Pro, Bell Stratos, Brancale SP4, Etto, Giro, Hanna Pro, Hanna Pro HP1, Kiwi, Land Tool Co., Maxon, Monarch, MSR, Nava, NJL Tour Rite , OGK, Securo, and Vetta. Helmets that have not passed the standards include Kucharik, SkidLid, Skidlid II, and SkidLid 1985. The Snell Foundation notes that "the safety of many of today's bicycle helmets is a dangerous illusion. In a crash, the rider can suffer similar injury or death as if no helmet were worn at all." Make sure that your helmet meets the standards. In addition to those listed above that did not pass, *all* leather hairnets and any helmet lined *only* with foam and no EPS, *will fail* and can cause permanent injury or death.

In addition to safety, an aerodynamic helmet, such as those seen in international competition since 1984, and the recent productions of Bell (the Stratos) and Monarch for the general public, can mean enormous savings in time. As Chet Kyle notes, "In a 25-mile time trial, use of an aero helmet would mean about a 30-second improvement in time. Almost all winning time trialists in international competition use aerodynamic helmets, including members of the Russian 100-kilometer, four-man time-trial team who set the current world record."

When riding in a pack of cyclists the safest place to be is toward the front. The better riders with more experience (and less chance of crashing) can be found there. If there is

A final piece of safety equipment is for the safety of the bicycle en route—the padded bicycle airline travel bag.

a crash, it will probably be behind you. The most common cause of crashing, especially for novice cyclists, is overlapping the front wheel with another cyclist's rear wheel. The trailing cyclist will always be the one to go down. Always keep an eye on the rear wheel in front of you. Other causes of crashes include wet corners in turns, improperly glued-on sew-up tires, a high-speed blowout, or just not looking where you're going (and thereby colliding with any number of inanimate objects). The key to safe riding is maintenance of equipment and awareness of the environment around you.

Regarding equipment, several regular checks will help prevent accidents. Make sure your sew-up tires are glued on properly, so that when dry they cannot be rolled off by hand. If you're riding sew-ups or clinchers, check for "bubbles," or a small area where the inner tube is showing through the sidewall of the tire—if there is such an area, the tube will likely blow that day. Check brakes, brake cables, derailleurs, and chain to make sure the mechanics of propelling and stopping the bike are functional. Also check the handlebars and stem—they should be tight enough so that with the front wheel locked between your legs you will be unable to move the handlebars in either direction, even when straining. It is important to note that if you don't check these things before a race, an inspector will. If there are *any* of the above problems, you will not be allowed to compete on that bike.

107

RAAM champ Pete Penseyres rides this aerodynamic human-powered vehicle to a new course record. (Photo courtesy of Tim Brummer)

"Why is it that champion racing cyclists can travel only about twice as fast as a recreational cyclist although they can produce nearly six times as much power? The answer lies in understanding the forces against a cyclist."

—Dr. Chester Kyle,
Founder, International Human-Powered Vehicle
Association

8
AERODYNAMICS

The force impeding a cyclist from faster speeds and higher performance is mostly air resistance. It has been shown that with speeds in excess of 18 miles per hour, 80 percent of the total force acting to slow the vehicle and rider is air resistance. Since little can be done to streamline the human body (other than losing weight and wearing aerodynamic clothing, both discussed in other chapters), the majority of work has been done on the design of the bicycle.

The first major innovations on the geometry of the bicycle frame were made in the late 1800s, when such designs as the "hobbyhorse," the "ordinary" (also known as the "high-wheeler" and "penny-farthing"), and the "upright safety bicycle" gave way to the drop-handlebar designed "racing" bike that positioned the rider in the crouched position. With the cyclist over the pedals and bent at the waist, the shoulder and chest area created less body drag. The changes from 1865 to 1900 were dramatic. But then a sanctioning body was formed that set up guidelines and limitations on future developments. In terms of overall

A straight-line drafting paceline with the wind coming directly from the front. (Photo by Dave Nelson)

geometry, the design of the bicycle has changed little since 1900. Frank Rowland Whitt, a historian of the technological development of the bicycle, argues that the bicycle had reached near perfection by 1900 anyway, and that future dramatic improvements were not possible.

To go faster cyclists quickly realized the value of the "draft." In drafting, or riding in the "slipstream" of another rider, as much as 30 percent in energy savings is realized. It has been shown in tests that four cyclists riding

A crosswind from the left forces the cyclists to move to the right for the ideal draft. (Photo by Dave Nelson)

in a paceline, taking turns at the front of the line while the others draft, can easily ride three to four miles per hour faster than a solo rider.

Carried to its extreme drafting can produce tremendous speeds. In 1899 Charles "Mile-a-Minute" Murphy rode one mile at the unheard-of speed of 63.24 mph, drafting a train on a board track specially built between the iron rails of a railroad line. In 1973 Dr. Allan Abbott rode a bike 138.674 mph on the salt flats of Utah behind a souped-up race car, a mark bettered by Ironman champion and Race Across AMerica veteran John Howard in 1985, when he exceeded 152 mph. It has been calculated that a cyclist could travel 238 mph at one-tenth of one horsepower on the moon, where there is no air and only one-sixth the gravitational pull.

The mechanics of the problem are straightforward. At 20

111

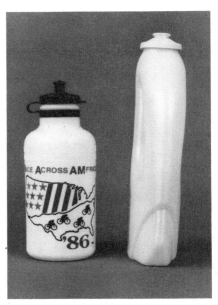

A profile shot of a standard water bottle, left, and an aerodynamic water bottle, right. The narrow profile of the aero water bottle prevents extra drag.

mph a cyclist displaces approximately 1,000 pounds of air a minute. This is called drag (and definitely *is* to anyone who has ever battled a stiff headwind). There are two basic types: *pressure drag* and *skin-friction drag*. Pressure drag occurs when the flow of air fails to follow the contour of the object pushing through the air. The separation of air, say around a standard water bottle, causes the air pressure at the back of the bottle to decrease slightly. This pressure difference causes more drag on the front, slowing the object's movement. A "teardrop" shape solves this problem by preventing air separation from occurring. The practical results of this finding can be seen in teardrop helmets, tubing, water bottles, handlebars, and rims.

Skin-friction drag, much less of a force than pressure drag, is related to shearing forces generated in the boundary layer close to the surface of an object. In other words, the smoother the surface, the smoother the air flow over it. The application of this principle can be seen in rubberized and lycra skinsuits, shoe covers, caps, and helmet covers, and in shaved legs and arms.

The pressure-drag principle also applies to spokes, each one of which causes a minute, yet measurable, drag coefficient. This has led to the development of bladed, or flattened, spokes, and the latest creation—the disk wheel. In the latter, the disk acts like a giant, single spoke, smoothly slipping through the air. Dr. Kyle, at the scientific cycling congress in Colorado, held in conjunction with the 1986 World Cycling Championships, reported that in a 25-mile time trial, riding at 25 mph, a cyclist saves the following amounts of time with the replacement of each standard component by a more aerodynamic one:

- aero frame—42 seconds
- aero spokes—39 seconds
- aero handlebars—29 seconds
- disk wheel—53 seconds
- aero water bottle—14 seconds
- aero shoes—14 seconds
- aero clothing—15 seconds
- aero helmet—30 seconds

The evolution of the bicycle wheel. From right to left: 48 spokes, 18 spokes, 1 spoke. The fewer spokes, the more aerodynamic the wheel. The Wolber Discjet can save as much as 53 seconds over the 48-hole wheel over 25 miles at 25 miles per hour.

It has been shown that for speeds in excess of 18 miles per hour, 80 percent of the force acting to slow the vehicle and rider is air resistance. This problem is tackled with a wraparound fairing. (Photo courtesy of Ron Skarin)

This adds up to almost four minutes in one hour of riding. These effects are dramatic, considering that most races are won or lost by seconds. Extrapolated to the 3,150-mile Race Across AMerica, taking into account speeds below 20 mph, approximately four hours could be saved by using the above equipment. Certainly part of Pete Penseyres's 1986 record-breaking performance of eight days, nine hours can be accounted for by his strategic decision to adapt these latest developments.

The laws of aerodynamics explain precisely how and why it is so difficult to ride fast through air. The power necessary to propel an object through air increases by the cube of the velocity. In other words, a modest increase in speed requires a monstrous increase in power. At 20 mph, a cyclist suddenly doubling his power output will only reach 26 mph. Add headwinds to the formula and the effect becomes even more pronounced. At 18 mph a 10-mph headwind will require a 100 percent increase in power just to maintain the same speed.

This problem was addressed in 1933 when Marcel Berthet of France rode 31.06 miles in one hour, three miles farther than anyone else had previously ridden in one hour on a conventional bicycle. Berthet's unconventional bike featured a wraparound "teardrop" canopy, which greatly reduced the pressure drag. Many creative designs followed, with corresponding increases in speed, but when the Union Cycliste Internationale banned all aerodynamic devices from competition in 1938, major innovation came to a halt.

Improvements were made in the componentry of the bicycle, including multigeared derailleurs, quick-release hubs, and so on. But overall speed increases mostly depended on the improvements in the riders themselves— until 1973. In that year Chester Kyle and Jack Lambie began work on measuring the reduction in drag that could be achieved through streamlining. Through their research they estimated that as much as 60 percent of air drag could be reduced with an enclosure. In 1974 Ron Skarin, an Olympic cyclist, set five world bicycle speed records at the Los Alamitos Naval Air Station. On April 5, 1975, the first annual human-powered vehicle race was held at Irwindale, California. Fourteen vehicles entered, with the kudos going to a streamlined tandem at 44.87 mph. By way of comparison, the fastest unaided cycling speed record was held by Russian Sergei Kopylov, one of the fastest cyclists in the world, at 43.45 mph.

In 1976 the Human-Powered Vehicle Association was formed, but the Guinness Book of World Records refused to recognize any of the recently established records because they were not sanctioned by an "international" governing body. So Chet Kyle added "International" to the name, and the IHPVA was born. Within a decade the speeds increased into the high 50s and low 60s. In 1986 Fred Markham, riding the Gold Rush II, designed by Gardner Martin of Easy Rider, Inc., reached a speed of 65.49 mph and won the Du Pont prize of $18,000, helping to defray the $20,000 cost of constructing the vehicle. The machine was a completely enclosed, streamlined recumbent that bore almost no resemblance to a standard bicycle.

Aerodynamics plays an important role in both competition and recreational cycling. For the competitor, more speed means a higher finish. For the recreationist, more speed almost always translates into more fun. Who doesn't prefer gliding along effortlessly, as opposed to laboriously struggling down the road?

At the end of the Great American Bike Race, August 15, 1982:
the moment of satisfaction after 10 days, 19 hours, and 54
minutes. (Photo by Christa Shermer)

PART III
THE
PSYCHOLOGICAL
EDGE

"Life can be so short,
you know everybody's bored.
So come on—move out on the highway,
get on down the road,
leaving it all behind.
There's been too much lying,
there'll be no more crying . . . this time.
Living on the edge,
running with the wind.
Soaring to the heights,
on an eagle's wings.
Living on the edge . . ."

—Jim Capaldi
"Living on the Edge"

Athletics are the great cultural equalizers. When you line up at the start of a ride or race, social status disappears. Occupation becomes meaningless. Upbringing and family name earn no favors. The doctor and the lawyer stand side by side with the artisan and tradesman—and no one can tell who is who. The varied roles and accompanying role uniforms are all traded in, and what emerges is a colorful band of brothers and sisters.

There is much more to athletics than meets the eye. Technology and physiology are only part of the game. The ability to psych up before a major event can and does affect performance. The satisfaction you get from your performance is more related to your mental attitude toward an event rather than the actual outcome. The balance between the physical and psychological is now known to be directly related to health and performance. The pinnacle, or "high," that is experienced in athletics is more than just endorphins and adrenaline. It's the feeling of completion and integration of one's self—physical, psychological, emotional, and spiritual—wrapped up into one package for one specific purpose for one period of time.

In this final section the three areas we will discuss are psychling, satisfaction, and pinnacle. They are subjects that are not as easily defined as those in the technological or physiological realm. They are, at times, subjective, coming from within. All personal experiences are just that, personal, and by definition cannot be quantitatively tested in a laboratory or objectively experienced by others. But the effects are real. We have all experienced the difference mental attitude has on performance. This effect may be likened to the judge's quandary in ruling on pornography—it's difficult to define, but you know it when you see it!

It would be difficult for any of us to put a finger on a particular event or day that changed our lives. There are many forces that shape personality and ego. But if I had to choose one day that was the turning point in my life, it would be Sunday morning, August 15, 1982. On that morning, 10 days, 19 hours, and 54 minutes after leaving the Santa Monica Pier in California, I reached the Empire State Building in New York City—by bicycle. Though I've now competed in four transcontinental bicycle races and numerous other endurance events, and my performances have been progressively better, that one day sticks out as my pinnacle.

It's a feeling that is difficult to define and impossible to measure. But it's there. Leaving Santa Monica I was an incomplete person. I had no idea what limitations on my capabilities might exist. I didn't even know if I could finish, let alone win. When I arrived in New York City I knew, for the first time in my life, a feeling of balance and harmony within. And it didn't really matter what happened after that first Great American Bike Race. Oh, I would get faster and stronger and better, but never more fulfilled. Not in the Ironman Triathlon. Not in the Spenco 500. Not in the Seattle-to-San Diego. Not in the Miami-to-Maine. Not in the San Francisco-to-Los Angeles. And not in any of the subsequent Races Across AMerica.

Everyone can experience this feeling, and it doesn't take racing across America. Whether it's riding 30, 300, or 3,000 miles, everyone has a time in their lives at which they reach their turning point. That is the essence of athletics in general, and cycling in particular.

Michael Secrest demonstrates supreme concentration during the 1986 Race Across AMerica. The ability to focus and concentrate is fundamental to achieving a goal. Too much, however, can lead one to become unaware of surroundings and competitors. (Photo by Dave Nelson)

"Only in games is man free, because only in games does he understand what is going on."

—Jean Paul Sartre

9
PSYCHLING

There is something special about games, sports, and athletics that seems to set them apart from life itself—the rules, guidelines, and boundaries are fixed, and there is a specific purpose and meaning to all actions. The game of life is unreliable. The guidelines are unclear. The rules are broken and punishment frequently avoided. The games of life, however, allow man a kind of existential freedom, as Sartre believed.

In athletics there is a special form of beauty, similar to but still unlike that found in other human endeavors. As philosopher Mortimer Adler notes in his book *Six Great Ideas*: "The enjoyment of beauty is not confined to the lives of those who have the habit of visiting museums, attending concerts or ballets, going to the theater, or reading poetry. It occurs also in the lives of those who are baseball, basketball, or football fans . . . . The sports spectator who, beholding an extraordinary play or action, cries out, 'Wow, that's beautiful,' is experiencing the same enjoyment or disinterested pleasure that is experienced by the auditor of a Beethoven quartet."

121

My love affair with the sport of cycling stems, in part, from being in love with something that is beautiful. In either watching or participating in a bicycle race, one experiences feelings of pure, unadulterated beauty. A cyclist descending a circuitous mountain road, or negotiating a hairpin corner, embodies the phrase "grace under pressure."

A PSYCHOLOGICAL NEED

This special form of beauty leads to a joy experienced by nearly all who ride a bike. I believe that it stems from a psychological need for physical stimulation in the form of exercise. Much like the innate need of physical stimulation through touch, humans need to experience physical exertion, a need inherited from ancestors whose very lives depended on such activity. There will be those, of course, who argue that "couch potatoism" is alive and well. I agree, but those people are deprived individuals who are missing out on an experience that can enrich their lives. Adler observes: "Pleasure itself, bodily or sensual pleasure, is among the goods that human beings desire. We have a natural craving for sensory experiences that have the quality of being pleasant . . . ."

THE MIND'S ROLE

At the scientific cycling congress in Colorado, Dr. Andrew Jacobs, president of The Winning Edge and sports psychologist for the U.S. Cycling Team (including and especially for the 1984 Olympics), noted that "the demand for a greater understanding of the psychological characteristics of athletes has occurred because it has been determined that mental training and preparation can be the major difference between athletes of equal physical ability."

Psychological research has determined that the most successful athletes are best at narrowing their attention under pressure. For example, in the individual pursuit the cyclist must be able to concentrate on pushing himself harder and harder throughout the race by focusing on a goal, internally on a specific time or externally on catching his opponent.

In my experience with the Race Across AMerica, both as a competitor and last year as an observer, the ability to focus during the race has been one of the deciding factors in the finishing position. Too weak an internal focus and you lose time to the distractions involved in crossing the country. Too weak an external focus and you lose touch with the world around you, both the physical environment and the competition.

In the 1982 RAAM Lon Haldeman was the most focused. He had twice ridden across the country the previous summer, was completely prepared physically and mentally for what was to come, and gave his complete attention to the task for nine days and 20 hours. Of the other four, John Marino had such painful saddle sores he couldn't concentrate on his cycling, let alone go fast. John Howard was completely unprepared for the boredom and fatigue, and found his mind constantly wandering from the race. For me, almost the entire 2,976 miles was a battle to keep my mind on the task at hand—riding to New York as fast as possible. The smallest distractions would cause me to get off the bike—change a music tape, get a massage, or argue with a crew member. Haldeman's focus led him to victory.

One of the most difficult aspects of any endurance event—such as the RAAM, a stage race, a long road race, or even a century ride—is maintaining concentration for the duration of the event. The mind tends to wander and lose focus on the task at hand—pedaling the bike as quickly as possible—which leads to a drop in speed. This is precisely why it is always better to train with others than alone. In a pack of riders who are sprinting for city-limit signs or just talking about cycling, the focus is maintained. When riding alone it is easy to be distracted.

Even on a climb, when the effects of drafting are at a minimum, once a cyclist gets dropped from the group his speed decreases significantly. And as they say in the sport,

"Out of sight, out of mind." If the competitor who is chasing loses sight of the leader, his speed is likely to decrease because he loses the concentration of focusing on something ahead. This is why a bike computer is a good idea for time trialing and century and double-century rides. It keeps the mind focused on a standard by which to judge performance—speed.

On the other side of the Atlantic, where the field of sports physiology was born and evolved to its current advanced state, Paul Kochli, director sportif of the professional cycling team *La Vie Claire* (including members Bernard Hinault and Greg LeMond), has taken an unexpected stand on the use of computers and sports physiology testing to train a cyclist to his peak. Kochli believes that all professional and top-level riders should be in charge of their training programs. Kochli teaches his cyclists to ask themselves questions about their bodies and how far they can be pushed. Ideally, the cyclist should be a combination rider and trainer. Since everyone is different, only the cyclist can really evaluate his performance. When pressed for the "magic formula" that has led to his team's success, Kochli demurred, saying there is no secret. The individual rider makes or breaks himself. He has to want to win, and then make the decision to do whatever it takes to reach that goal. Kochli stressed the importance of the mental or cognitive aspects of the sport, in addition to the physical, noting that each is important for a successful balance.

VISUALIZATION

There are many techniques for developing a working relationship between the mind and body. Every sports psychologist and trainer will have his or her unique method. There is one technique, however, that is common throughout sports psychology in particular and psychological therapy in general—visualization. For several years at the beginning of my cycling career I worked with a hypnotherapist who not only hypnotized me but taught me how to do visualization on my own, so that I would no longer need her skills. Her methodology consisted of three parts.

PART I. TENSION—RELAXATION

In this exercise the athlete learns what tension feels like in its extreme form, and then how it feels to eliminate it.

1. Sit on an easy chair or couch and feel relaxed and comfortable.
2. Clench your fist as tightly as possible for 30 seconds; feel it shake and note that the knuckles are white.
3. Relax your fist and *feel* the tension flowing out of your arm and hand into the air. As you note this feeling of relief, say to yourself, "Relax, relax, relax," over and over, until the association is made between the word "relax" and the feeling of tension relief.
4. Repeat Steps 2 and 3 again and again until the association is a strong one.

PART II. RELAXATION

In this exercise the entire body will learn the relaxation process.

1. Repeat the process described in Part I, only do so for all the major sets of muscles in the body.
2. Begin with the toes. Curl them up against the balls of your feet, hold it for 30 seconds, relax them, and repeat to yourself, "Relax, relax."
3. Move up to your ankles, calves, thighs, stomach, back, arms, shoulders, neck, and finally facial muscles. Repeat Step 2 with each of the muscle groups until you feel you have complete control over your body's muscular system.

PART III. VISUALIZATION

In Part III the system used in Parts I and II is applied to a specific situation.

1. Visualize yourself in a situation that is anxiety pro-

ducing, such as at the starting line of a big ride or race. Try to feel what that tension and anxiety is like.

2. As you slip into that tension and anxiety, immediately say to yourself, "Relax, relax." If you have been practicing Parts I and II, the tension and anxiety should disappear.

3. Repeat this sequence over and over until you feel you have mastered your fears and anxieties.

4. Mentally place yourself in other situations that are anxiety producing and repeat the above steps.

In psychology this is known as "progressive relaxation," or "systematic desensitization," and is commonly used in therapy for phobias and anxiety attacks. It is based on the principle of pairing imaginary anxiety-producing scenes with the genuine state of physical relaxation. Because anxiety and relaxation are incompatible responses, anxiety responses decrease as relaxation responses increase. These pairings are made in a hierarchical order, beginning with the least anxiety-producing scene and gradually progressing until the terminal scene, the most difficult situation, can be imagined without any feeling of anxiety.

When I was working with the hypnotherapist, she had me imagine myself on a television screen on which I could observe myself in various situations, such as at the beginning of the Race Across AMerica, riding through the 115-degree desert heat, climbing long and steep mountains, descending without fear, overcoming boredom, riding with pain, and so on. When I was in the actual race I could call upon my mental imagery at any time and see myself successfully negotiating the problem.

Certainly visualization is not the only key to overcoming psychological problems in your performance, but it is a useful technique that anyone can learn; and while a therapist is ideal, it can be practiced with this simple three-part program.

It is always easier to maintain focus when the competition is in sight. In a rare moment in ultramarathon cycling John Marino and I ride together outside of Dalhart, Texas, a situation that inspired me to ride considerably faster than if I had been alone.

Michael Secrest shows classic climbing form—out of the saddle, hand on the hoods, rocking the bike back and forth, and throwing his body weight into each pedal stroke. If you want to become a strong cyclist fast, climb, climb, climb. (Photo by Dave Nelson)

"I don't want to gain immortality through my work. I want to gain immortality through not dying."

—Woody Allen

10
SATISFACTION

Exercise *is* the most important thing anyone can do. And not just for the prevention of disease and postponement of deterioration. The quantity of life is transcended by the *quality* of life. Through a consistent exercise program, you will not only live longer but the quality of those extra years will be improved. I recently tested my projected lifespan on a computer program that asks the user questions from which it can determine, through insurance actuarial tables, answers to the probabilities of a long life. Available on software adaptable to Apple and IBM personal computers, the program can determine your actual equivalent age, taking into account all possible variables of living styles, including the amount of exercise per week. I was pleased to discover that my actuarial age, or my projected lifespan, is that of an eleven-year-old. The computer program also informed me that if I were to lose another five pounds, it would lower my actuarial age to 10. If the average life expectancy (the expected age at which the average individual would die, taking into consideration accidents and disease) of the American male is 70.8 years (78.2 for females), I should have another 60.8 to go, provided I lose that extra five pounds! (The computer program is called Health Risk Appraisal, and is available from HRM Software.)

Studies show that those who expend at least 2,000 calories a week exercising (approximately 100 miles of cycling) are more likely to reach the age of 80 than those who expend less than 2,000 calories a week. Statistically, 68.2 percent of men aged 35–39 who burned at least 2,000 calories a week are expected to live to the age of 80, while only 57.8 percent of subjects who burned less than 2,000 calories are predicted to live that long. Between age 40 and 70, for every hour you exercise you will gain two hours of life. By exercising three hours a week for 30 years, a 40-year-old will live an an extra 9,360 hours, or 390 days. I don't know about you, but I'll take the extra hours. It's worth the work, especially if it is an enjoyable form of exercise, such as cycling.

THE TAO OF CYCLING

"Be bent, and you will remain straight.
Be vacant, and you will remain full.
Be worn, and you will remain new."
—Lao-tzu

In the sport of cycling there is a balance to be found that can make for a more integrated, holistic, and healthy existence. When riding a bike there is the interaction with nature and all of her elements—heat, cold, sun, wind, humidity, rain, hills, valleys, and so on. There is also the balance that exercise gives an otherwise sedentary lifestyle. Exercise and rest. Hunger and satisfaction. Pain and pleasure. Climb and descend. Peaks and basins. Highs and lows. Tear down the muscles in order to build them up stronger. Increase your heart rate in order to slow it down. Raise your blood pressure in order to lower it. Taper down in order to go hard. The yin and the yang.

As Lao-tzu taught, opposites attract. Going in the opposite direction will get you to your destination. "Be worn, and you will remain new" is especially fitting in the world of athletics and cycling. I have never felt more new than the day after an intense workout. Exercise is so habit-forming that I feel old if I miss a workout session.

CYCLING AS A WAY OF LIFE

What has all this to do with cycling? To achieve health, both physical and psychological, we clearly need an approach different from the one we were raised to believe would make us whole. While I am not necessarily suggesting a complete conversion to "mystical" Eastern philosophies, a different "way" to lead a more balanced life is worthy of consideration. My personal bias leads me to emphasize a balance through exercise. Obviously my preference is for the sport of cycling—the Tao of cycling, if you will allow me to adopt an overadopted inscription. A steady diet of cycling on a daily basis can lead to a more integrated and healthy lifestyle, for all the reasons previously discussed—both physical and psychological. Whether the bicycle is your vocation or avocation, cycling can be a rewarding and satisfying *way* of life.

One of my colleagues at Glendale College, Dr. Richard Hardison, recently related a story to me about Frank Holman, a friend of his in Hawaii. This older and wealthy gentleman was once one of the chief executive officers of a major aerospace manufacturing company. He had money. He had power. He even had a 747 at his disposal for travel. Upon his retirement he moved to the big island of Hawaii, where he invested in a macadamia nut farm. It's a profitable business, though he didn't really need the profits. One day Dr. Hardison visited his friend and found him out in the hot lava-bed field, sweating and toiling to harvest his macadamia nuts. "Couldn't you just hire someone to do the hard labor for you?" Dr. Hardison asked. "I suppose so," Holman replied. "But I suppose I could hire someone to play my tennis for me as well!"

One of the most difficult aspects of any exercise program is consistency. There are many summer soldiers and sunshine patriots in the world of sports. The weekend athlete abounds in every sport, cycling included. Health clubs and insurance companies bank on the fact that people will not be consistent in their strivings to be healthy. But as any exercise physiologist will tell you, consistency is the fountainhead of any exercise program. It is far better to exercise one hour a day, seven days a week, than it is to exercise seven hours, once a week. The trouble for most people is that it is difficult to set aside one hour every day.

The key to maintaining fitness through a consistent exercise program is to have reasons, call them excuses if you will, to get out and ride. Every single day think of some reason to go for a bike ride. Make your own list as I have done. Meet the club for the weekly ride on Wednesday evening, or Tuesday and Thursday mornings. Set a time to rendezvous with a friend at a street corner or landmark away from home, forcing you to go or be inconsiderate. Make your trip to the bank or post office on your bicycle, not in your car.

If you're single, a great date is a casual bike ride on the weekend. It's a perfect opportunity to get to know someone without all the pressures of dating. If you're married, a bike ride can become a weekly ritual of shared activity when the schedules of work and chores interrupt normal interactions (and tandems are ideal for this). If you are concerned with cosmetics, a bike ride is a great way to work on your tan while improving muscle tone. If you work within a reasonable distance of home, and showers are available at the workplace, think of the money saved by commuting by bicycle, not to mention the health benefits from the ride.

One of my favorite reasons, or excuses, for cycling is to meet a friend for a ride. We will set a time and place to meet away from either of our homes, with the mutual guilt complex of not wanting to appear unreliable as our motivation to show up for the ride and to be on time. Despite my reputation for having a slow-running clock, I have never failed to at least show for the ride, late or not. This system also works well when meeting a friend for breakfast or lunch at some designated restaurant a good distance from your home. Since eating is such a powerful reinforcer for most people, especially aerobic athletes like cyclists, this trick works well.

I try to make all my trips to the bank, post office, or food market by bicycle. A sizeable day pack will carry a reasonable amount of goods when running errands. Even some business meetings, especially those not requiring formal dress, can be reached by bicycle. Whenever I participate in other sports, such as tennis, racquetball, or running, I ride to the event. For all sports a proper warm-up is essential, and a bike ride is a perfect way to accomplish this. I recently entered a racquetball tournament at the local YMCA, and arrived at the final championship match by bicycle. My opponent, not being a cyclist, was a bit startled to learn I had ridden "all the way from Hollywood" (about 18 miles). This may have even contributed to my victory!

Satisfaction comes from being happy doing what you must do. You must breathe, eat, earn a living, and so on. Why not choose to breathe fresh air, eat wholesome foods, and enjoy the job? Why not choose a life of health and fitness? As top triathlete Scott Tinley says: "Challenge yourself when you race, sure, but be aware of the total picture as you do. The real point of this whole thing for 99 percent of the people involved is maintaining a healthy, superfit lifestyle."

The effects of aerodynamics are demonstrable and powerful in John Howard's amazing land-speed record of slightly more than 152 miles per hour. (Photo by Al Gross)

"Try not to become a man of success but rather try to become a man of value."

—Albert Einstein

11
PINNACLE

Throughout this book I have been discussing the various ways to improve performance. Physiologically, technologically, and psychologically, there are many different avenues to success. But there is a common thread that runs through the three major sections and 11 chapters of this book— setting goals to accomplish what you would like to achieve. In order to be a high achiever, you must integrate the physiological, technological, and psychological into a holistic blend of body, machine, and mind. Setting goals is the means to that integrated end.

Writing down a goal restructures your thinking from "I wonder if I can accomplish it" to "I wonder how long it will take me to accomplish it." Having the goal down in black and white drives you beyond your present limits.

The higher you set your goals, the greater your accomplishments—whether it's a world record, a triathlon, winning a race, making money, getting A's in school, choosing a mate, selecting a job, or just striving to be happy. If you aim to make $50,000 a year, for instance, you will perform at a much higher level than if the goal were $25,000. Even if you fall short of the goal and only earn $35,000, you've still accomplished a lot more than you would have with the lesser goal.

The process of writing down your goals can have an almost magical effect on reaching them. By way of analogy, when you go out to run errands for a few hours, if you haven't written down all the different places you want to go, you may not only forget a few stops but the pattern of driving around may not be as efficient as it could be if the route were planned in advance. This is how goal accomplishment works. If you write your goals down, you'll get everything on the list, and then some. I carry a notebook with me everywhere I go (with the exception of riding a bike). Whenever an idea strikes me I write it down. If I remember I need to call someone, I write it down. I have a list for everything and every day. I have a short-term list and a long-term list. I get the list out every morning and look it over to see what I'm going to do that day. I even keep a pad of paper and pen next to my bed so that when ideas strike as I'm dozing off, or in my sleep, or as I awake in the morning, I write them down (memory is fleeting in these altered states of consciousness).

THE BACKWARD APPROACH

If the project is an extensive one, such as preparing for a major athletic event—a stage race, the Ironman Triathlon, the Race Across AMerica, it is best to write down all the things that have to be done, in a specific fashion—backward. I always use the backward approach to all projects and events. I count backward from the scheduled time of the event to the day I will begin training, calculating how much time I have and how much progress I want to make. For the 1985 Race Across AMerica my goal was to ride over 330 miles a day, every day, for nine days. The race was scheduled to begin July 19, 1985. I began my serious training rides in March, allowing five months to build up to triple centuries. I started with 25-mile rides, then 50-mile rides, progressing to 100, 150, 200, 250, and finally 300 miles in one day. As each distance is mastered, it becomes easier to be able to cover it at any time. If you have mastered the century ride, then 50 miles is easy, 100 miles is natural, and 150 miles is challenging. The more miles ridden, the easier it becomes.

WINNING AND LOSING

Selection of high goals should be made within the boundaries of physical, intellectual, and mental possibility. In selecting goals that are unattainable, the ensuing frustration could lead to negative side effects. There are two ways to win a race. You can be first across the line, or you can have done your absolute best. When Vince Lombardi said that winning isn't everything, it's the only thing, he was correct; but it all depends on your definition of winning.

To win is to perform at the highest level you are capable of reaching, to use every resource available to you, to give 100 percent of your energy and effort to the task. If it happens that someone else has also done this and his or her capabilities are higher than yours, then there is only one conclusion: you both won. Your opponent just happened to cross the line ahead of you. Your respect for that person, and for yourself, should be elevated.

At the close of ABC's "Wide World of Sports" program on the 1982 Great American Bike Race—the forerunner of the Race Across AMerica—Jim Lampley ended the show with the following statement that reflects the above view of winning and losing:

"I speak for Diana Nyad and everyone in our ABC Sports production crew in saying that this event was the most strenuous, the most tedious, the most difficult to cover of any we have ever been involved with. It was also the most rewarding. The trip that seemed to have started a century ago was finally over, 12 days later. We had seen four very extraordinary athletes lay their very different souls and personalities open to the bone. And we had seen them all finish. It goes without saying that in this event winning and losing turned out to mean very little. And that is exactly the way it should have been."

INDEX

Boyer, Jonathan, x, 40, 69, 79, 96
Brake levers, 58
Burke, Ed, xv, 12–13, 15, 63–64, 66
Buttocks, 53–54

Campagnolo, 76
Campbell, Arthur, 73
Carbohydrates, 65–67
Carbo loading, 66
Cardiovascular system, 8
Cavanagh, Peter, 27, 28–29
Chainring, 84
Clincher tires, 93
Clothing
    choice of, 48, 95–101
    color of, 94, 100–101
    and comfort, 33, 95
Coles, Michael, 41, 42, 45
Comfort, 49–61
    importance of, 50
Computers
    on bicycles, 85–86, 89
    program for analyzing
        quality of life, 129–30
Conconi, Francesco, 5, 10, 14
Consistency, in exercise
    program, 132
Costill, David, 63, 68–69
Cotton clothing, 98
Cycling
    as exercise form, 50
    sport of, 72, 131–33
    as way of life, 131–33
Cycling deaths, 105
Cycling gloves, 56
Cycling shoes, 51
Cycling shorts, 54, 97
Cyclog, 21–25
Cyclogistics, 21–22

Deltoids, 42
Derailleur, 73, 80
Dips, 35
Disk wheel, 90, 113
Downstroke, 27–28
Drafting, 110–11, 123–24
Drag, 112, 114
Drivetrain, 81

Eat to Win (Haas), 63
Einstein, Albert, 135
Endorphins, 9–10
Endurance, 8
Energy transfer, 69
Equipment, safety of, 107
Exercise. *See also* Training;
    Weight training
    cycling as form of, 131–33
Eye protection, 96

Fast-twitch/slow-twitch ratio, 32
Fats, 65, 68
Feedback, 21
Feet, 51
Finger push-ups, 46
Fingers, numbness of, 55
Fit Kit, 53, 60
Freewheel hub, 73

Gear-inches, 83
Gearing, 8085
Gear ratio chart, 85
Glycogen, 11, 68–69
Goal setting, 135–36
Goggles, 102
Gore-Tex, 99–100

Haas, Robert, 63
Haldeman, Lon, x, xi, 3, 15–16, 74, 89, 91, 98, 123
Haldeman, Susan, 89
Handlebars, 57
Handlebar stem positions, 56, 57–58
Hands, problems with, 55–56
Health Risk Appraisal, 130
Heart, 7
Heart-rate monitor, 5, 6, 10, 11, 21
Heiden, Eric, xviii, 2–3, 68
Helmets, 104
    manufacturers of approved, 106
    safety standards for, 105–6
Hemoglobin, 13
High-altitude training, 14–18
Hills, techniques for climbing, 16–18, 128